Born in Leeds in 1935, Barry Cryer attended Leeds University where he read English, but was more interested in performing. His professional debut was at the famous City Varieties Music Hall and from there he went on to the, now legendary, Windmill Theatre in London.

By Barry Cryer

Pigs Can Fly

You Won't Believe This But:
An Autobiography of Sorts

with Humphrey Lyttleton, Graeme Garden
& Tim Brooke-Taylor
The Little Book of Mornington Crescent

with Humphrey Lyttleton, Graeme Garden,
Tim Brooke-Taylor & Willie Rushton
I'm Sorry I Haven't a Clue
The Almost Totally Complete I'm Sorry I Haven't a Clue
I'm Sorry I Haven't a Clue: The Official Limerick
Collection

with Richard Webber, Bob Larbey & John Esmond
A Celebration of the Good Life

Pigs Can Fly

BARRY CRYER

ORION

An Orion paperback

First published in Great Britain in 2003
by Orion
This paperback edition published in 2004
by Orion Books Ltd,
Orion House, 5 Upper St Martin's Lane,
London WC2H 9EA

A CIP catalogue record for this book is available
from the British Library.

ISBN 0 75285 919 6

Printed and bound in Great Britain by
Clays Ltd, St Ives plc

www.orionbooks.co.uk

Introduction

The letter lay on the table. To be fair, it was all it could do. 'Dear so-called author,' it began. I was hooked. Removing the hook upon which I had impaled myself, I sat down to read it. The letter, not the hook.

'Whilst surfing the net,' it continued, 'I stumbled upon the information that you are the author of a book entitled *Pigs Can Fly*. I managed to obtain a proof copy of this work – I am not at liberty to divulge how, suffice to say I have contacts.' I have always eschewed contacts, so I donned my glasses and read on. 'Not to put too fine a point on it, the anecdotes that you relate are a tissue of lies, a farrago, pure mendacity, fabrication, counterfeit, falsification …' Pausing only to reflect that the writer was a keen student of Roget, I read on. 'The fact that you have the gall, the effrontery, the chutzpah …' oh dear, here he goes again … 'to pass these stories off as true, defies belief. I see no reason why a gullible public should be subjected to what is obviously pure fiction masquerading as fact.'

'Yours, Oliver Roberts'

I carefully filed the letter in the bin. Oliver Roberts? My mind raced, searched the recesses of my memory. And then it came to me. 'Smelly' Roberts, Leeds Grammar School, 1948. A boy ostracised by his fellows – firstly on the grounds of his overwhelming halitosis, as indicated by his far-from-unsubtle cognomen and secondly his habit of whipping you in the shower with a wet towel. Even then we realised he was a sadomasochist. The masochistic side of his nature was obvious – he loved a cold shower, but always took a hot one.

I told him about the letter. 'Publish and be damned,' he cried, quoting the late Duke of Wellington. A man who also said, of his own army, 'I don't know what effect these men will have on the enemy, but, by God, they terrify me.' So be it. And so, Oliver Roberts, wherever you are, do your worst – or wurst if you're in Austria. Every word in this book is true, with the exception of a few adverbs. All my sources can be verified, as indeed can all my sauces.

Dear reader, trust me. Read on and you be the judge.

Barry Cryer, *News at Ten*,
The Priory, September 2003

For Graham Chapman's memorial, they couldn't find a church big enough, so they hired the Great Hall at Bart's Hospital, where Graham had studied, and it was an amazing day. I was the MC, as requested by Graham one afternoon in hospital. John Cleese was rather miffed that it wasn't in church because he said he'd always wanted to say 'fuck' in church, but he did a hilarious address about Graham which was full of abuse, demonstrating a complete lack of reverence, but was wonderful and got big laughs. He did say 'fuck' quite a lot, and then went off. And I said, 'Thank you John, that was fucking marvellous,' and introduced Michael Palin. Michael came on and said, 'Being the third one to say "fuck" today hasn't got much going for it, not much of a cachet!' At the end Neil Innes, wearing his duck hat, sang 'How Sweet to Be an Idiot' and there wasn't a dry eye in the house. Eric Idle then bounced on and got the whole audience to sing 'Always Look on the Bright Side of Life', shouting all the while, 'I can't fucking hear you!' What a day that was.

Another night to remember was at the Theatre Royal, Stratford East. Peter Cook had been in full cry in the bar, and on stage he began to harangue the audience about Tottenham Hotspur football club. John Junkin and I were sitting behind him on the stage, and the great Cook was whipping the audience up into a frenzy. They were actually laughing and booing at the same time, and Junkin turned to me and said, 'Let's strip!' We duly did, behind Peter, to much applause. Emboldened by this applause, Peter reached new heights and we had to keep stripping to the inevitable conclusion.

Like everyone who knew him I have great memories of Peter Cook, but not all of them are happy ones. I worked on the ill-fated *Joan Rivers Show* at the BBC. We recorded six shows in seven days, and Joan had announced at a late stage that she wanted a Brit sidekick rather on the model of Johnny Carson, who had Ed McMahon as his cohort. This has been much copied since. We have Jonathan Ross on the radio with Andy sitting next to him, Terry Wogan with his producer, Paulie Walters, Mark Lamarr and Mark Steele – it gives you a partner to bounce ideas off. So now Joan had asked for Peter Cook, and this was virtually a *fait accompli* because the series was looming when the demand suddenly came and Jim Moir, then the Head of Variety at the Beeb, and my friend Neil Shand, were deputed to acquire Peter Cook. At the time this was very good news for Peter and his agent, David Wilkinson. Peter was signed up for, I'm sure, a lot of money. The trouble was that in practice Peter just did two or three minutes at the top of the show before being relegated to the end of the settee. Now a man of his calibre doesn't get going in two or three minutes, so this was a painful experience for him each and every recording night. He was then sent right down to the end of the settee and usually addressed with questions that only demanded the answer yes or no. This was a shameful use of that great character and I remember in the middle of the series getting a tearful phone call from him in the early hours of the morning. I don't flatter myself – he was probably doing a ring round – but Peter was in tears, saying 'More people have seen this fucking show than anything I've ever done.' This conversation was very painful for both of us.

The night Bernard Manning appeared on *The Joan Rivers Show* was one to be remembered. Joan started the show by interviewing Russell Grant, the astrologer, who had announced his refusal to appear on the same screen as Bernard Manning, so Russell was just going to do his interview and leave the building. My old friends Dick Vosburgh, Neil Shand and a gang of us were upstairs in our writing room, which had been converted into the guest hospitality room, and a whole army of friends of Joan Rivers – blue rinses and whatever from Los Angeles – came in to drink and chat. Erupting into the room came Bernard Manning in shirt and braces, who greeted us

– 'Hello Dick, hello Barry, hello Neil' – and sat down under the rather astonished gaze of the Los Angeles visitors. On the screen, the show had started, and Russell Grant was on with Joan Rivers. 'What's that poof doing on television with professionals out of work?' blurted Bernard Manning. 'Oh my God!' said a woman behind him. So I thought, 'The evening's getting off to a roaring start.' Then Bernard went downstairs to get ready for the show, and soon he came on. Joan had obviously never heard of him, she must have thought he was a sort of English Don Rickles, a provocative comedian, which is a not inaccurate definition of Bernard but not the whole story. Then Bernard looked down at Peter Cook on the other end of the settee. Peter had had another painful experience at the top of the show doing his two or three minutes. Bernard said, 'Saw you at the top of the show, Peter, very funny,' and then pulled a face into the camera. The atmosphere was electric by now and we staggered through the recording. Joan was aghast at what Manning came out with, and at the end of the recording, cameras off, Rupert Everett, who was another guest on the show, nearly went for him, physically, with Peter saying, 'Hold me back, hold me back!' and not moving.

Zero Mostel was the original lead in the American production of *A Funny Thing Happened on the Way to the Forum*, and I heard the story about him and George Abbott, the amazing producer/director who lived to be about a hundred and who was directing *Forum*. During a rehearsal Zero Mostel suddenly snapped, hurled a torrent of abuse at the immaculate Abbott, who was standing in the stalls, and then stormed off the stage. Somebody else, astonished that this eminent man would put up with such abuse, said, 'Why did you let him get away with that?' George Abbott just said, 'Actors! Who listens?'

Joan Littlewood, the Queen of Stratford East, and an absolute heroine of mine, told me that she was once in the lift at the Savoy Hotel. She was a little woman, woolly hat and tennis shoes, as she used to say, and she was in this lift at the Savoy and she realised the large man she was in the lift with was Zero Mostel, one of her heroes. And she thought, 'I wonder what floor he's getting out on. I can't waste a moment like this,' and she looked up at him and said, 'I'm Joan Littlewood' – and he looked down at her and said 'So am I!'

When *A Funny Thing Happened on the Way to the*

Forum was coming to London, the lead was to be played by Frankie Howerd. Prior to this, Frank had had yet another of those dips in his career, which was like a rollercoaster. His career was one long series of comebacks, and I remember going to see him in Coventry, where he was in a pantomime but wasn't even top billed – Sid James was top of the bill. This was when Larry Gelbart and Burt Shevelove, who wrote *A Funny Thing Happened on the Way to the Forum*, were wondering who to have as the lead in London, and they were talking to John Gielgud who said, 'Oh, you should get Frankie Howerd.' And they went to that same pantomime in Coventry and, sure enough, they thought, 'This is the man!' Auditions were held at the Strand Theatre in London. I was working with Danny La Rue at Winston's nightclub at the time and we were doing *Cleopatra* because the film had just come out, with Danny playing Cleopatra, obviously, and me playing Anthony. I had a breastplate, toga, boots, helmet and everything. So, having purloined my costume from the club and smuggled it home, and having got to bed at about four a.m., I went down to the Strand Theatre the next morning. I found a dressing-room by the side of the stage and changed into the toga and the helmet and the breastplate and all that and I thought, 'What can I do? This is a sort of vaudeville, music hall show combined with ancient Rome.' So I sang an old song

'That Was a Cute Little Rhyme', thinking how clever I was, and they said, 'Thank you, we'll let you know,' but they never did and I didn't get the part. Years later I met Larry Gelbart at a party and I told him I'd auditioned for *Forum* in London. He said, 'Oh, I didn't get to any of the auditions, Burt did the auditions,' and we talked about that and he said, 'Burt told me some idiot came on one morning with a breastplate, a toga and a helmet on.'

I came to know and admire the comedian Arthur Askey very well indeed. He was a man who was obsessed with now. He never looked backwards unless you asked him to and then he would tell great stories. He was always looking around the current scene and always up to date with everything, and he once said, 'Every generation's the same, a load of crap and a few brilliant people.' I've never heard a better definition. He and Richard Murdoch had been big stars before the Second World War in a radio show called *Bandwagon*. Two men, very dissimilar in styles. Dickie Murdoch's background was the Cambridge Footlights and Arthur's was Masonic dinners and the concert party. Two very distinctive voices, great radio performers, but you could hear Arthur ad-libbing, wandering off the script, which is enormously impressive, and when he became a television star after the Second World War, the same thing applied. He would talk to the camera, he would obviously mess around with the script trying to throw his fellow artists, and I admired him very much indeed. One of my great unfulfilled ambitions was to record an April Fool show for BBC Radio with Arthur Askey and Richard Murdoch, whose voices still sounded just the same. The premise of the show would be that we would have band arrangements in period, as in the Forties, somebody who could conceivably have been in the show with them then would be in it – and that would have been Maurice Denham, who died only recently – and the tape would be degraded or scratched up a bit so that it sounded exactly like 'Discovered in the BBC vaults, the hitherto unheard show with Richard Murdoch and Arthur Askey'. Then in the middle there would be a Margaret Thatcher joke. They were up for it, and I treasured the idea of somebody listening at home and thinking, 'Did I hear that?' But Arthur got ill and it was terrible because he then got gangrene in one leg, which had to be removed, and I went to see him in St Thomas's Hospital in London and he was laughing.

At the height of the Jubilee frenzy my old friend Clive Dunn, he of *Dad's Army*, rang me from

Portugal, where he now lives, and said they'd been watching the celebrations there on television. He told me that seeing the Mall full of thousands of people took him back fifty years to the coronation and reminded him of a joke told at the time by Arthur Askey: a triumphantly pregnant woman was standing in the crowd watching it all go on and a man said, 'You all right?' and she said, 'Yes, I'm fine'. Then he said, 'You look magnificent,' and she said, 'Oh, thank you.' Then she said, 'It's twins,' and the man, just to make conversation, said, 'What a pity they can't see all this,' and she said, 'Well, I've taken my knickers off so they can hear the band.'

I've done a good deal of after-dinner speaking and performed at awards ceremonies and conferences and so on, and I was thinking about the smallest and the largest audiences I've ever spoken to. Once, years ago, I was at a hotel near Dartmoor, for what I took to be some sort of business conference for a car hire company. I arrived, as per usual, went to my room, had a shower, put my suit on and went down to the bar. There were several men in the bar and we talked and I met the managing director, who had arrived by helicopter. I think there were eleven of us, all told.

Dinner was at eight o'clock, and as the time approached I said to the managing director, 'Where's everybody else?' and he said, 'This is it, this is the audience.'

'What?' Nobody had told me. So we went in to dinner and all eleven of us sat round one big table, and in due course the managing director stood up and charmingly introduced me, but I didn't stand up. Instead I said, 'The speech is cancelled,' and the look on his face was amazing.

I said, 'No, no, this is ridiculous. I've just been with you all in the bar. Standing up and addressing you would seem phoney. Look, I'll tell a joke, and then,' I said, pointing at the managing director, 'you tell a joke. I'll try and match it and we will go round the whole table.' The group around the table included two, I have to say, very shy men, but this is what we did. I told a joke, the managing director told a joke, I told another joke and pointed at one of the guys and he told a joke and then it was my turn ... We went round the whole table and, suffice to say, the dinner finished at three o'clock in the morning and there were no complaints whatsoever, and even the two shy men came out of their shells. It was a very good session, and the only time, to date, that I really haven't done what they expected me to do when I arrived.

Dick Emery told me that he got back from holiday once and he and his wife were literally unpacking when his agent rang and said, 'Somebody's dropped out. Get down to the Savoy Hotel, there's an after-dinner.' So Dick said, 'Yeah, that's fine,' jumped in a taxi and went down to the Savoy. He'd been told who to ask for at reception, and this man arrived and took him to one of the dining-rooms in the Savoy that are named after Gilbert & Sullivan operettas. When he got to the Pinafore Room there were just six people, and that was Dick's audience, and he did something similar. He just sat there and told jokes and talked to them, and there were no complaints at all. So you never know what's going to happen.

At the other end of the scale Willie Rushton and I once played, or spoke, to ten thousand people at the London Arena for a charity. They told us how Pavarotti had played there and was unable to get to the dressing-room they'd prepared for him because the corridor was too narrow. They swore it was true. He had to have a room with a rather wider approach, shall we say. That reminds me of what I always say about telling jokes – what a dangerous game it is. After all, when Pavarotti starts singing 'Nessun Dorma' nobody shouts, 'Heard it!' We went to a Pavarotti concert last year actually … he doesn't like it when you join in, does he?

I flew to Guernsey years ago on a Wednesday to do an after-dinner speech for a company I'd worked for before, and subsequently worked for again, but I'll never forget that day! The sun shone out of a clear blue sky, the plane landed, and I was met by a charming woman, went to the hotel, into the ritual, up to the room, showered, put the suit on and I went down. What I witnessed when I got down was rather akin to a Hogarth painting. There was shouting, rowing, deafening noise. They were all drunk out of their minds. There had been redundancies in the company and a lot of internal politics that I knew nothing of, and the mood was distinctly ugly. Two men were conducting a raucous commentary for a large Scalextric runway that had been set up on the floor of the bar, and they were doing all these private jokes with a lot of obscenities and people were laughing a lot and one man said, 'You'd better be funny to follow these two.' All this was not raising my spirits. I then went into the dinner, where the noise level rose. Bread rolls were being thrown about, somebody was sick on the carpet and eventually I was introduced, practicably inaudibly, because of this wall of noise that was coming. I stood up to speak to merry cries of words beginning with C and W and all I could do was just plough on. I did much less than I usually do, probably about ten or fifteen minutes, which is a long time when nobody's listening or they are shouting abuse. I then sat down, but it was rather as if nothing had happened. I was just a man in the corner of the room. But there's always nice people around, and two guys took me to the bar and one said 'That was disgusting' and bought me a drink. In the end we stayed up all night and I missed my plane in the morning. I got home finally and I was working again that very night in Norwich. My self-confidence was now reduced to rubble on the floor. I'd never felt so apprehensive, but I went to Norwich and met three hundred delightful people and got back on course again.

It was a good, busy week, and I was very lucky. On the Friday I was in Glasgow doing an awards ceremony with a thousand people, and had a very happy night telling jokes and ploughing through all these awards. Afterwards a man loomed out of the darkness and said, 'Hello, you won't remember me. I was in Guernsey on Wednesday. So this is what you're really like!'

Humphrey Lyttelton was once being interviewed on Radio Clyde in Scotland, at a time when he was writing about restaurants and food in addition to all his band and radio activities, and the interviewer said, 'Mr Lyttelton, I believe apart from your jazz and your food writing you're a very keen orthinologist,' and Humph said, 'Surely you mean word-botcher?'

Now I thought that was great, but when I asked if he said it he replied, 'Actually I thought of it on the way home – I wish I *had* said it then.' I believe it's what the French call *l'esprit d'escalier* – staircase wit. You're just leaving a gathering and you think, too late, 'Oh, I should have said that.'

In my anecdotage, I talk to Humphrey quite a lot. We're both rather notorious (me certainly) for launching into anecdotes at the drop of a word. My friend and writing partner, Ray Cameron, used to say to me, 'I wish just once I could mention something that doesn't remind you of something else.'

The master of anecdote was, of course, David Niven, who would actually relocate stories and recast them to make them neater and funnier. For example, he'd think that one would be funnier if he said it wasn't about him, and another would be better if it was set in Paris. As a counter-balance to David Niven's monster bestseller *The Moon's a Balloon* Sheridan Morley subsequently wrote a biography of David called *The Other Side of the Moon*. It wasn't a hatchet job, he was just correcting one or two things, saying no, here's what actually happened, and it's fascinating to read those two books in tandem. Now the point I'm making is that Humph and I often talk about telling stories and the way, after you've honed them and polished them, you begin to wonder if they're actually true. I always claim that I spoke to

Marilyn Monroe on the phone, but then I began to think, 'Did I really, or have I psyched myself up into thinking that?' I told Humph about this and he said, 'Well, I've been saying for years that when I was a young subaltern in the Guards I played my trumpet outside Buckingham Palace on VE night. But I began to be slightly troubled by the thought: is this story true, or have I just convinced myself it's true?' He told this to his band, and two of his musicians who are radio buffs did some research and obtained a recording of a BBC commentator outside Buckingham Palace on VE night and in the background you can hear Humph playing 'Roll Out the Barrel'. They gave Humph this bit of tape as a present, and he said he was deeply touched. He just played it and thought, 'It's true!'

Anonymity fascinates me. Some people are just invisible or unrecognisable, even though they're basically famous. I've just been to the memorial service for my friend Peter Tinniswood, the writer, and Paul Schofield slid into a seat in the back pew at this memorial. I'd worked with him in 1958 in the musical *Expresso Bongo*. Since 1958 I've met him about three times and each time it's as if we'd met yesterday. He remembers where he met you last time and so on, but this man shimmers in and out and we spoke briefly after the service in the sunshine outside and suddenly he was gone. He shimmered round the side of a white van that was parked there and was gone. It's the opposite of charisma. This great actor can just make himself invisible and yet he's got a very definite face. It's not like Alec Guinness not being noticed with his mask of a face; Paul Schofield is a very definite-looking man, but seems to make himself invisible.

Years ago, through my in-laws, I met and spoke with a charming man with thick white hair and horn-rimmed glasses who turned out to be Charlie Cairoli, the famous clown. Well, he of course was never asked to sign an autograph in the street in his life. Thanks to the red nose, the moustache and the hat that he used when performing, he was unrecognisable when he walked around, because without make-up he was a distinguished-looking man with white hair and glasses. Warren Mitchell, whom I've known for years, can be almost as anonymous. In between series of *Till Death Us Do Part*, Warren tended to grow a beard and wear a black leather jacket, and you could walk down the street with him and nobody would recognise him at all, even though this was Alf Garnett, one of the most famous faces on television. With Clive Dunn, who always had very young hair, and still has, it's the same thing.

With a leather jacket, horn-rimmed glasses and his young hair, he's rarely recognised in the street. It's a sort of gift. I know you want to look after the public, and if someone comes up to Warren or Clive and asks for an autograph, they will be quick to oblige, but if people don't it leads to a very peaceful life. I am fascinated by this anonymity, this strange form of invisibility.

On the subject of clowns, there's a wonderful story about the great clown Grimaldi. He was prone to depression and went to see a psychiatrist, and they talked of this, that and the other and finally the psychiatrist said, 'You need a laugh. Go and see Grimaldi,' and he said, 'I am Grimaldi.'

Amnesty International asked me to take part in a series of readings from the works of writers who were in prison. I chose Jeffrey Archer. That's a joke, but it brings me to the lovely Archer. I do a lot of after-dinner speaking, and a lot of it consists of jokes, which are of course in the public domain. The audience just hear jokes, but we, all of us, at some point, write some material for ourselves and I had a particular section – five or ten minutes' worth – that was known to be mine and that's what I did ... Anyway,

I went to a lunch at which Jeffrey Archer spoke and could not believe my ears as he launched into this section practically word for word, and I was furious. But I thought, 'I don't know what I'm going to do about it.' After the lunch I was walking out of the hotel and I heard footsteps behind me and it was Jeffrey Archer. 'Barry,' he said, 'I changed it a bit in the middle. What do you think?'

I was standing in a buffet at Paddington Station one night and looked at the man next to me, who had white hair and glasses like me but was infinitely more handsome, and I thought, 'That's Cary Grant.' He toyed with a half of lager or something, then he looked at his watch and left the buffet, and I suddenly put two and two together. There was the Bristol train, and I knew that whenever Grant was in England he used to visit his mother in a home in Bristol, and I said to the barman, 'That was Archie Leach' – this being Cary Grant's real name – which was fatuous of me, and it didn't register with the barman at all. But it does remind me of two stories. One took place years ago at The Palladium, where my friend Alfred Marks and his wife Paddy O'Neill were playing the king and the queen in a pantomime and the buzz went round that Alma Cogan, the singer, was going to be in that night accompanied by Cary Grant. Cary Grant knew Alma's family. So the buzz went round and they duly saw the show and everything, and the next day Alfred Marks sent Alma Cogan a telegram saying, 'Couldn't you find a nice Jewish boy?' There's an irony here, because years later a man called Charles Higham wrote a book in which he revealed that Cary Grant was half Jewish, so the joke was only half true.

And this, in turn, reminds me of Roy Hudd's story. He was performing in Bristol, and one afternoon when he hadn't got a matinee he was walking through the hotel lounge and he saw Cary Grant having tea. Roy's like me, he doesn't let moments pass, so he walked over and said, 'Hello, I'm Roy Hudd,' and Cary Grant said, 'I know you are, you're in the pantomime. I'm coming to see it tonight.' So he sat down, had a cup of tea with Cary Grant and they chatted and then Roy went off to the theatre. The place was abuzz with excitement. 'Cary Grant's in tonight,' people were saying, but Roy blanked everybody out and said, 'Oh, come on, where have you heard that? That's ridiculous.' After the show they were all asked to go into the green room backstage and line up as if for a royal presentation, and Cary Grant walked in and said 'Hello, Roy'. Roy said he'll treasure that moment for ever.

My old dear friend Alan Coren is one of the genuine wits of our day. Alan didn't tell me this story, somebody told this story about him. He was having lunch with a man one day and the man said, 'I'm going to order artichokes. Never had artichokes at all. I'm going to order them. A new experience.' So the artichokes duly arrived and the man looked at them and said, 'Alan, I don't know anything about artichokes. What are these?' and Alan looked at them and said, 'Today Jerusalem, tomorrow the Globe!'

Awards are a constant motif in these reminiscences. I was once at the Royalty Theatre for the Olivier Awards and the great man, who was a good age then and not too well, was attending. He and his wife Joan Plowright, and family and Gawn Granger, the actor, were all in a rather nice little suite behind a box at the Royalty. You went straight into the box from this room, which had a television set, a drinks cabinet and its own loo and everything. I was on the stage doing the warm-up and, as I was later told, it was thought it would be rather a good idea to sort of smuggle Larry into the box in the dark quietly while I was doing the warm-up, so that there wasn't a great kerfuffle with him being confronted by bright lights and everything. I was telling a joke which, leaving modesty aside, went rather well with the audience and some people actually clapped at the end of it. It happened to coincide exactly with the moment that Laurence Olivier entered the box, and even in the dark he raised his arms to receive this accolade. His wife said, 'Sit down, he's telling a joke.' It's the only example I can point to of an incident involving me and Laurence Olivier.

If that sounds like a fairly distant encounter, I had a closer one with the legendary Harry Saltzman, of Saltzman and Broccoli, makers of the James Bond films. Harry had acquired the rights of a cartoon series about Sherlock Holmes and Moriarty and Father Christmas, which he thought could be the new *Peter Pan*, and he offered me the job of adapting it for the theatre. I honestly thought it had all the makings, so I did my adaptation, making out that Watson was the real brains behind the outfit and Holmes was a fraud (an idea that was subsequently used in a film with Ben Kingsley), and that Father Christmas didn't really like children. My agent, Roger Hancock, brother of Tony, said 'Do not let Harry have this script until we've got the contract sorted.' On my way to see Roger one day I had lunch with Billy Connolly and Ray Cameron, my partner in writing Kenny Everett's shows, to talk about Billy's appearance on the show. We were sitting in Langan's Restaurant in London and who of all people should walk in but Harry Saltzman. The script, which I was taking to Roger's office to be locked securely in a safe, was in an envelope leaning against the leg of my chair. Harry Saltzman looked across the restaurant, waved a greeting and then came over and we introduced him to Billy Connolly. He chatted very pleasantly, and then he looked at the envelope. Now he couldn't have known, it was just a shot in the dark, but he said, 'Oh, is that the script?' and I heard my voice saying 'Yes' and he picked it up, thanked me and went off with it. When I reached my agent's office sans script, he said 'Well, where is it?' and I told him what had happened. His reply was short and of a four-letter word nature. I think I may be the only man to be mugged by Harry Saltzman.

I can never remember which Bond film it was in where Sean Connery said 'Q, you're a shite for shore eyes.'

There is this story that any sighting of a butterfly at the Theatre Royal, Bath, brings good luck and a dead butterfly, obviously, the reverse. Willie Rushton, who was performing there with me, heard about this and was enchanted with the thought. We went out for lunch one day before doing a show at the theatre and Willie noticed some butterflies in a case on the wall and asked if he could borrow one of them, which he then set up in a little frame. Our show opened with me on the stage telling jokes, and I related the legend of the butterfly to the audience while behind me Willie wandered on and showed this framed butterfly to the audience, crying jovially 'Got the bugger!' After the show one of the crew said to me, 'Never mock the butterfly!'

'It wasn't me,' I said, 'it was Willie.'

Not long afterwards I appeared again at the Theatre Royal and I had a message at the stage door saying that my mother had rung. As my mother had been dead for several years I wondered what her extension was, but the woman at the stage door said, 'Oh, she said she was your mother,' which was a bit creepy. After the show my wife and I went to Leslie Crowther's house, in Corston, outside Bath, to stay with him and his wife Jean. We were shown up to our room, and there on the radiator was a dead butterfly and my wife said 'Your mother's popped in.'

The butterfly is reputed to have landed on the

head of Peter O'Toole at Bath during rehearsals of *Jeffrey Bernard Is Unwell*, and that show subsequently became an enormous hit, with many productions, including a revival with Peter, so you be the judge.

Willie Rushton was prone to having a conversation with his cat after breakfast. It was a big fat cat, I remember, because I often used to go to his house in Earls Court. One day Willie said, 'I was talking to my cat the other morning, chatting away about current affairs and topical matters, lovely morning, sunny, the window was open and suddenly a moth fluttered into the room. "Good morning to you," I said, and the moth alighted on the settee. I chatted to the moth for a moment or two and then the moth, either having a prior engagement or being bored, flew out of the window. I turned to my cat and I said, "I'm going mad. I've just been talking to a moth!"

In the circus, the clowns are the great understudies, the great substitutes. They can all do maybe a bit of trapeze and a bit of balancing and a bit of juggling etcetera. They can do a bit of everything, so if there's a crisis you ask one of the clowns to fill in. There's a story I like in which the boss of the circus says to the clown one day, 'The lion tamer's broken his leg, you're on tonight.' The clown says, 'I'm not going in a cage with those.' 'Come on,' says the boss. 'You've seen the act a hundred times – the lions do the act, you just stand there posing.' So the clown says, 'OK, OK, but I'm doing it, not you. Just for the sake of argument, what if they come down the tunnel, they go on to the stools and one of them starts to improvise and comes off the stool and comes at me?' And the boss says, 'Well, crack the whip, they can't bear it, he'll go back.' So the clown says, 'OK, OK, what if I've cracked the whip and he still comes at me?' 'In the left-hand pocket of the costume there's a pistol loaded with blanks. Fire it in the air, he'll go back, they can't bear that.'

Then the clown says, 'Forgive me, just hypothetically, you know – this is all happening, I'm going to do it tonight – I've cracked the whip, he's coming, I've fired the pistol, he's coming, what do I do then?' The boss says, 'There's a cane chair in the cage, you've seen that. Jab the legs at him, they can't bear it, he'll go back.' The clown is still not sure and he says, 'OK. I've cracked the whip, he's coming, I've fired the gun, he's coming, I've jabbed the chair at him, he's still coming at me. What now?' And the boss says, 'Well by now, I should think, you'll be against the bars of the cage. Reach behind yourself and throw a lump of shit in his face.' The clown says, 'Will there be shit behind me?' And the boss says, 'Will there be shit behind you??!!'

While we are on circus-related stories here's another of my favourites. There's this circus boss – for the sake of argument we'll call him Circus Boss. His doorbell rings one day and there's a man standing there carrying a hold-all bag and he says, 'Mr Circus Boss? Can you give me five minutes of your time?' So Circus Boss asks, 'Why, what is this all about?' The man says, 'I've got something that might interest you for your circus.'

So Circus Boss lets him in and the man says, 'I am the man who feels no pain.' 'What are you talking about?' Circus Boss says, whereupon the man opens the holdall and there's a sledgehammer in it and he says, 'Hit me over the head.' And Circus Boss says, 'I can't hit you over the head, that's ridiculous.'

'But I am the man who feels no pain.'

So, trying not to overdo it, Circus Boss taps him gently on the head with the sledgehammer and the man collapses. Panic breaks out, Circus Boss rings for an ambulance and the man is taken to hospital. He is in a coma for about three months, and nearly every day Circus Boss goes in, tortured with guilt and remorse, and sits by the bed. One afternoon three months later he's sitting by the bed and the man suddenly wakes up with a triumphant look on his face and goes 'Tara!'

The character actor Arthur Mullard became a friend of mine. He was a big man with a wonderfully lived-in face, an archetypal cockney, who looked like an old boxer – I think he had boxed when he was younger – and had some lovely stock lines. Whenever he was booked to do a show, for example, and the cast sat round the table for the read-through of the script, he would invariably say to the director, 'D'you want this cockney?' He once played Virginia Woolf on television, which is another amazing story.

Arthur once made an unforgettable appearance on *Midweek*, the Radio 4 Wednesday morning programme, now hosted or hostessed by Libby Purves, known to everybody at the BBC as Nurse Purves for reasons I've never quite gleaned. Victor Lewis-Smith, now an acerbic columnist for the London *Evening*

Standard, used to be a radio producer, and he thought it would be funny to have Arthur Mullard hosting an edition of *Midweek*, with Roy Hudd and me among the guests. Victor was right, because Roy and I could hardly speak for laughing as Arthur, holding his script within an inch of his nose, bellowed questions at the guests. The programme had what we call talkback, in other words the producer could talk to the studio, but the novelty here was that this was broadcast as well, live, so the audience could hear the producer talking. At one point Arthur was interviewing somebody and suddenly Victor's voice cut in: 'Arthur.'

'Yes?'

'Ask him how he started.' Click.

And Arthur said to the guest, 'How did you start?'

There was another click and Victor said, 'Yes, something like that.'

The world of coincidence. I was in Hanover Square at about half past five one afternoon. The whole world was heading towards Oxford Circus, hundreds of people milling around or making their way to the tube, and I was talking to a guy, very vehemently and angrily, about an actor I knew who'd given a woman friend of mine a very hard time physically as well as verbally. He was an absolute bastard, and as I was in full flow about this actor to the man I suddenly stopped talking. 'What's the matter?' he said. I said: 'He's just walked past.' True story.

Once as I was on my way to Birmingham by train to do a show for ATV – *New Faces*, with Marti Caine – there was some trouble with the loco and we were all decanted at Bletchley. This was in pre-mobile phone days and I was worried, so I went into the booking hall and a man said, 'You look worried. What's the matter?' and I told him. He said, 'Come into the office and use the phone.' So I rang ATV and told them I was going to be a bit late and they said that would be OK. In fact they were bringing another train and I would soon be on my way. I went back on to the platform into this heaving mass of people and I was standing next to a besuited man with a briefcase. He turned to me and said, 'I've always wanted to meet you,' and, as I started to preen myself, he said, 'My name's Barry Cryer as well' and produced ID.

One day before a recording of *I'm Sorry I Haven't a Clue* the cast were sitting around and Humphrey Lyttelton said, 'I've been asked to write a magazine article on coincidences.' Instantly feigning surprise, I said, 'So have I!' You can't miss a feed line like that.

Having spent many years of my working life with comedians, I'm always intrigued, sometimes enraged, by their erratic behaviour. They have a skew-eyed view of life and, with the best ones, you never know what they're going to do. I worked with a comedian called Jimmy Wheeler, who used to play the violin and wore a patently false moustache under his very colourful nose. He and the grape were not strangers – he liked to drink. I met him at the Sheffield Empire, near to my home town of Leeds. The Empire theatres were the big ones, what they used to call the Number Ones, and they were in every big town and city, but this was the only one I ever worked in. On that bill was Mr Wheeler, with his violin, and the amazing Chic Murray, who was then doing a double act with his wife, Maidi. I was in awe of these people and when, after the music rehearsal, Jimmy Wheeler invited me across the road to the pub for a drink, I thought, 'Well, I'd better be careful here – this man is a legendary toper.' He bought me a pint and then he bought himself a half of bitter, and I thought, 'Oh, this is interesting, all the stories are untrue.' But after a half, his demeanour changed and I realised sadly that it was straight into the bloodstream and he was just tuning up again. Having said that, he never failed to do his act. That very night there was a lot of trouble in Cyprus with EOKA and Archbishop Makarios and everything, and Jimmy Wheeler departed from his act and delivered a speech in which, to the astonishment of the audience and the band, he sang the praises of our brave boys in Cyprus before finally getting back to his jokes. As I say, you never know what they are going to do.

Years ago, at the Hippodrome Theatre in Coventry, I was told that Peter Sellers, at the height of his *Goon Show* fame, came on to the stage there with a chair, a folding card table and an old wind-up gramophone. He then proceeded to put on a 12-inch LP, as you used to call it, of Christmas carols, saying to the audience, 'These are lovely.' They were all baffled, of course, and remained so as, instead of doing his act, Sellers sang along with the carols. There was a drama about it, but I think he managed to survive the rest of the week. That night he must have just felt like singing along to carols.

A story about Tommy Cooper that I heard after Tommy died. He did his army service in the Guards, I think it was the Lifeguards, and the story goes he was on sentry duty outside the box, standing legs astride with the rifle, and he fell asleep standing up. After a while he half-opened an eye and in front of him were the regimental sergeant major and his commanding officer. 'Oh,' thought Tom, and closed the eye. And after a pause he opened both eyes and said 'Amen'.

Thanks to the Lord's Taverners – and the Lady Taverners, our paramilitary wing – I became acquainted and even played cricket with some of my idols. Giants of the game. In particular Denis Compton and Bill Edrich. Bill would have a large gin and tonic on the shelf in the changing-room prior to going out to bat, and Denis would turn up at matches wearing a dinner jacket after being up all night. Peter Parfitt, a Middlesex team-mate of theirs, relates a story of Denis arriving wearing a dinner jacket and falling asleep. He was half awake as they dressed him, padded him and got him ready, after which he said 'Anybody got a bat?', then went on to the field and scored 129 not out. This is not recommended to younger players as a *modus operandi*.

The Lord's Taverners used to hold their dinners in the Napoleon Suite at the Café Royal in London, and one year they were going to hold a joint dinner – not a meal where the smoking of joints or spliffs was practised, but a joint dinner for Bill and Denis – and they asked me to speak. I was very nervous about this. 'I need some raw material,' I thought, so I rang the Taverners office for the CVs of these great men. I had a rough idea of their careers, obviously, but I wanted some detail. So they sent me a mass of stuff and I sat looking at it thinking, 'OK, but what am I going to do with this?' Now where the thought came from I'll never know, but I thought I'd do a poem – 'Once more unto the pitch, dear friends, once more' – and I cobbled together this poem, rhyming couplets, no more no less, and did it that night at the Café Royal with Denis Compton on one side of me and Bill Edrich on the other. It was rather daunting to say the least. But these two old pros sensed I was reaching my climax and to my surprise and shock as I was reaching this orgasmic moment they both grabbed a hand of mine and swung my arms up in the air at the end of the poem. Nobody took a photograph – would that they had – but that moment remains in my memory. Also because it gave me the idea of doing poems at dinners.

In the late Seventies some of us Lord's Taverners would be contacted and asked to go on cruises on the *Canberra*, as sort of Redcoats really. A whole gang of us would go and play table tennis and do raffles and auctions and shows and all sorts of things on these cruises, and it was a very pleasant diversion. One day the sun shone out of a clear blue sky, hundreds of passengers gathered round the pool and much water sporting went on, with me as the commentator. And there was a Polish man on board who had come on alone and had become notorious on the ship. He'd blown what money he had on this cruise and was known to stay up all night in various bars and was just working his way round the ship in a state of ecstasy. Now Taverners are jumping in and out of the water, there was water polo going on and God knows what, and this man came up to me, naked to the waist but wearing trousers, and said he would like to swim a few lengths for the Taverners. I said yes, thanked him for that and thought, 'Well he's a bit older, but we'll keep an eye on him.' I thought he would then remove his trousers revealing trunks or whatever, but he just hurled himself into the pool to merry cries and applause from the audience. Looking back, it was a very insensitive commentary from me. I remember distinctly saying at one point, 'He's doing a sponsored drown for the Taverners' and various remarks of that tasteful nature, and then a hush descended because he was just floating, face downwards, and then Roy Kinnear did a great belly flop into the pool and pulled him out, but he was gone, blue in the face. The sun shone, hundreds of passengers stood very still, and then they were all taken away and we had to recover from that incident.

The cruises abounded with stories. Deaths do sometimes occur, sadly, and with married couples I was told there was a routine. If the man passed away on the cruise, the surviving partner would be given the choice: 'Shall we put him in the fridge till we get back to Southampton? Or would he have preferred to be buried at sea?' One story they swore was true was that a man died suddenly and his widow said he should be buried at sea – that's what he would have wanted. Now the ritual for burying a passenger at sea took place at the crack of dawn, really early, before most of the passengers were up. Crew members and musicians were selected by a rota system. One morning they were getting ready to see this poor man off and he was in a shroud on this mechanical device that would tip him into the water. Unfortunately the Master at Arms, who was in charge of the whole thing, accidentally knocked the lever with his elbow and, before anything had taken place, with a loud splash the man went into the sea. Nobody had come, they hadn't had a ceremony, and he'd gone! The Master at Arms, a master of lateral thinking, very quickly said, 'Go up to the galley and get a sack of potatoes.' So the potatoes were brought and arranged on the device under a reasonable facsimile of the shroud, then the sorrowing widow and the chaplain and the congregation arrived, and words were intoned before he was consigned to the deep. The lever was pulled, but what the small audience then heard was not one splash but two, the potatoes having been in two separate sacks which had come apart.

The other story I heard was that a man died and

the day after his death his widow appeared in the purser's office and said, 'How does this affect our raffle tickets?'

I once did two nights of cabaret on the *QE2* with a friend of mine, Barry Bignold, a pianist. Just as we were about to leave Copenhagen harbour, some of us were invited up top by the Captain to witness the leaving. It was a glorious, glorious summer day and we were all up there, drinks in hand, and as the massive vessel left the harbour it slammed into the jetty, nearly crushing a tug. We were then all asked to go below immediately and, as we went below, we heard the Captain saying on the tannoy, 'Some of you may have felt something, this is nothing to worry about' – which sounded like him thinking, 'My job's on the line, it hangs by a thread.' The *QE2* was newly refurbished and it had already hit the harbour in Copenhagen. And there we stayed.

I was the chairman of a nostalgia quiz called *Those Wonderful TV Times* on Tyne Tees Television and my friend Tim Brooke-Taylor came up to do one and Ray Allen, the ventriloquist, was booked, and he arrived without his doll, Lord Charles. This caused some consternation. They'd assumed they'd booked both of them, but Ray said, 'No, you booked *me* for this, not me and the doll.' There was a bit of an inquest in the producer's office, but then it was a *fait accompli*: they'd just got Ray, and he was glad to be there in his own right. So before the show in the green room, or the hostility room as it's sometimes known, Ray unwound quite violently, and he was networking and rushing around the room and telling stories and laughing and really getting into a very extrovert mood – through sheer relief that everything had been resolved – and as he was talking away to somebody Tim Brooke-Taylor leaned over to me and said, 'It's the drink talking'.

Norman Evans, a northern comedian, was another great performer I worked with. Norman did not enjoy good health. He'd been badly injured in a car crash, and although he'd recovered he still had quite a lot of difficulty walking, so they always managed to get him a dressing-room near the stage. I remember one time when we were at the Alexandra Gardens, Weymouth, and we were both smoking, and he introduced me to Consulate Cigarettes, menthol cigarettes, which in fact featured in the Stanley Kubrick film *Full Menthol Packet*, but that's neither here nor there. You could smoke in most theatres in those days, but the Alexandra Gardens was all wood, so understandably they had strict rules about smoking. Norman and his wife had a little Calor gas camping cooker and she'd cook sausages, and there would be the smoke from Norman's and my cigarettes and the smoke coming off the cooking sausages ... and there's a photograph of us and we're in the theatre standing underneath a No Smoking sign – totally irresponsible.

Norman was an idol of Les Dawson's, as was Frank Randle, the other great northern comedian, and you can see it in Les's work. Les was a great original but he was inspired by Norman. Particularly Norman's drag act, where he would be this loquacious woman talking to an invisible neighbour over the garden wall and would keep slipping and banging one of his boobs, at which he would exclaim, 'Third time this week on the same brick!' You had to be there. He was an amazing act.

Drag has been a constant motif in my career, because my start in London was with Danny La Rue, writing his nightclub shows and lines like 'I never wear women's clothes. Well, unless they fit!' Danny could come out with some lines. He was very shrewd because he played it very butch. 'Wotcha, mates,' he used to say when he came on, looking a million dollars. Men liked his act and women adored it, but men just thought, 'He's laughing, he's larking about.' We were having a drink with some customers in Danny's club one night, after the show, and this lady was all over him. 'Oh Dan, that was wonderful,' she said. 'Do you enjoy dressing up as a lady?' He said, 'No dear, do you?'

On the subject of drag, I've come to know Paul O'Grady, also known as Lily Savage. We were doing a show at the Hackney Empire, and in the next-door dressing-room Paul had a load of friends and family and there was quite a volume of noise emanating from the room. So I walked straight into his dressing-room without knocking and there was Paul as Lily, standing eight feet tall in his high heels, and I said, 'Some of us are trying to get ready for this show and we would appreciate a bit of peace and quiet and a bit of professionalism,' and Paul looked at me and said, 'And we don't really enjoy interruptions from sad old has-beens who are insecure.' We then started this monumental row, and we must have done it far too well because they were all looking at us in astonishment, jaws dropping, as Paul and I railed at each other, and then he suddenly beamed at me and said, 'Well, anyway, give us a kiss!' These are moments I treasure.

The old artist called Dougie Byng, who lived to an amazing age, had been quite a star in his day. He used to sing 'Nobody Loves a Fairy When She's

Forty' and other amazing, very camp songs like that. Dougie's speciality was to do drag without being in drag: he'd be wearing a dinner jacket but then would throw a feather boa round his neck and transform into this waspish woman. In 1996 there was a celebration at Alexandra Palace in London of the sixtieth anniversary of the BBC. I was deputed through my friend, Patrick Newley, to be Dougie's minder that day. So I picked him up and we drove over to Alexandra Palace together. He was rather deaf by then, but we had a merry time, talking away. Then we sat and watched a screening in black and white of cabaret at the Café de Paris in the Thirties, and there was Dougie. The audience were spellbound, knowing he was there and everything, but suddenly a voice at the back of the audience said, very loudly, 'Why are they showing this crap?' People turned round, in some shock, and it was Dougie Byng. He regarded it as not worthy of consideration. When the film finished, he announced rather loudly, 'I want to piss.' So I took him downstairs to the gents. Dougie proceeded to unzip his flies and pee into the washbasin and Patrick said, 'Dougie, you know the thing is over there.' 'I am an actor,' replied Dougie Byng.

I did a show at a hospital in Poole with my old friend Roy Castle. Years before I had been out of work. Roy Castle, who'd now become a star, was at The Palladium and he knew I was out of work but, typical of the man and his style and sensitivity, he said to me 'Oh, you're so busy but I do need a dresser at The Palladium, somebody to look after me.' He made it seem as if he was asking a favour from me, so I gratefully accepted. I was not one of nature's dressers. One night after the show I went off to a club called Gerry's in Shaftesbury Avenue, a legendary club where the game Mornington Crescent was actually born. After finishing two shows with Roy I went off with my friends the King Brothers, the musical act, to Gerry's and we had a very good time. Then Roy Castle suddenly entered the club, saw me and said, 'You got my car keys?' There they were, in my pocket! What a dresser. Anybody else would have lost their temper with me, and quite rightly too, but not Castle. He laughed, had a drink and left, then walked back to The Palladium, got his car, and went home.

Fast forward to the hospital in Poole where I did a show with Roy, who was not well by then, but typically had honoured an agreement to appear in this show. He wasn't meant to do an act or anything, but he suddenly decided, seeing me there, that he would get up and do some tap-dancing. Then he began to tell the story of me as his dresser and the car keys. I was standing in the wings, next to one of the musicians, and I said to him, 'Give me your car keys, quick!'

'What?'

'Give me your car keys, I'll look after them, I'll get them back to you.' So he gave me the car keys and just as Roy said, 'And I went round to the club and I said, 'Where are my car keys?'' I walked on the stage, brandishing these car keys aloft. Couldn't believe it, but the moment worked.

Roy's classic story was about the time when stardom first struck him and he was at The Palladium. Each night at the end of the show he would dash up Argyll Street and down into Oxford Circus tube, take the Bakerloo Line to Marylebone and catch the last train back to Denham, where he was then living. One night after the usual dash he was on the train and got into the compartment, where people were sleeping and reading, and just before the train left, the door opened – one of the old carriages with the doors you could open yourself, great safety hazard but there we are – and a man got in. He was an archetypal city business-man, but his hair was askew and there was a stain on the shirt. He'd obviously been out on the toot for the evening and had just made the train home. He put his briefcase and his umbrella and his bowler hat in the rack, sat down and went to sleep and the train set off into the night. Then, as trains always do, for no apparent reason it lurched to a halt. Kajunk! And this guy woke up, got up, took his stuff down from the rack, opened the door on the embankment side and stepped out into the night. And Roy said, 'We were all very British, nobody said anything,' and then, he said, after a pause the umbrella suddenly came back on its own, then the evening paper, then the briefcase, then the bowler hat, then the man's left hand, then his right hand and then his face appeared, covered in muck from the embankment, with a burgeoning black eye and a bit of blood on the nose, and he climbed back into the compartment, shut the door behind him, bent down, picked up all his stuff. By now everybody was staring at him, and he looked at the assembled company and said, 'You must think I'm a terrible fool' – and stepped out the other side.

Here's a bizarre tale, told to me by the actor Michael Elphick, who sadly is gone now. He was working as a relief barman at the Burgundian pub in Finchley

Road in London, and one lunchtime a very tweedy lady came in and ordered a large gin and tonic. When he quoted the price to her she said, 'Oh no, have a word with the landlord,' so he said to the landlord, 'She's telling me to speak to you,' and he said, 'Oh, that's Dorothy, that's all right.' So, as we used to say, it was chalked on the board – she subsequently had three large gin and tonics and each time it was chalked up and she never paid and she left and Michael told me he came back in to work again that evening and a man came in, a bald man with glasses, and said to the landlord, 'Was Dorothy in this lunchtime?' The landlord said, 'Yeah, she came in,' and the man said, 'Oh dear, what's the damage? What did she have?' and the landlord said, 'Three large gin and tonics' and quoted him the price, which the man paid. It was him! He used to come into the pub at lunchtimes, in drag, dressed as Dorothy. True story. I said to Michael Elphick, 'We've got to do this as a television playlet or play,' and he said, 'Yes, we've really got to do this,' and I said, 'Maybe at the end of the play, the man comes in at night and asks how many drinks Dorothy had and pays the bill and, while he's doing it, Dorothy walks in behind him.' Spooky.

There was an act which, for the sake of argument, I will call Del Monte and his Dancing Duck. This was an ornithological act, with birds playing football, running up and down ladders, walking on tightropes, swinging on trapezes, and the climax of the act was a duck tap-dancing on a biscuit tin. I am not making this up. The spotlight would hit the duck and it would tap-dance. I couldn't have enough of this act, I used to watch it a lot and one night we'd had all the trapeze, tightrope, football, running up and down ladders and everything, then came the big moment. The spotlight hit the duck standing on the biscuit tin and it just stood there staring at the audience – complete anti-climax, music played, very little applause, act down the plughole and I was with the great Monte in the bar afterwards, or Reg as we knew him, and I said, 'What happened to the duck tonight?' and he said, 'Oh, the candle went out.'

There is a story I like about a young agent in America who later went on to become head of a large agency. Towards the end of Elvis's life when he was somewhat bloated – in his Las Vegas stage – you could still get him if the money was right, and the singer's notorious manager Colonel Parker got a call from this guy saying he wanted to put Mr Presley on in Miami at this particular arena or stadium. Parker said, 'Show me a million dollars as a token and we'll talk.' So the man got some credible evidence of financial backing and the upshot was that the agent put on Elvis Presley in Miami. Now Colonel Parker had said, 'Mr Presley does not appear in front of a single empty seat,' and on the day there were about two hundred seats unsold. Anybody else would have 'papered it', as we say, in other words dished out complimentary tickets to fill these two hundred seats, but time was of the essence and instead lateral thinking was used to solve the problem. The agent simply had two hundred seats removed and replaced by a bank of flowers. He was even complimented by Colonel Parker for this nice touch. That is what I call thinking swiftly.

The same man, by now very famous, was handling John Denver when he came over to Britain to do a tour. When they heard back in the States that Mr Denver was not happy with what was happening on his British tour, our man contacted Denver directly and said he was coming over personally. He arrived at some ungodly hour at Heathrow and was met by

John Denver himself and he thought immediately, 'Well, if Denver's here at this hour of the morning, we've got a problem.' He immediately wheeled into action. He said to John Denver, 'Wilson, who organised this tour, is gone, he doesn't work for me, he doesn't work for anybody, the man is finished, I have taken over. We will sort out the problems. Wilson has gone. Have no worries on that score.' Denver now started to back-pedal, asking about this man Wilson, whether he had a family and so on, and was feeling a bit bad about a man losing his livelihood, but this was brutally dismissed: 'Wilson has gone.' There was no such person. He invented him and fired him.

I knew Rod Hull – and his emu. Rod wanted to be a writer and performer generally, but in a children's programme in Australia he inherited the emu. The running joke for children was an emu egg hatching out on a radiator, and then of course the producers had to debate what was to happen when the egg actually hatched and somebody mooted the idea of a hand puppet of some description. And I think we all remember what happened, Rod took over the role with the dummy right arm and his right arm as the emu, which seemed to have a life of its own. I speak with some authority as I was 'emued' on one occasion by Rod, and however hard you tried you became convinced the emu was real. I walked into a rehearsal room once and Rod was sitting reading the London *Evening Standard* with Emu on his arm, why I'll never know, also perusing the newspaper. As I walked in, Emu looked up suddenly and fixed me with his baleful eyes and it was an uncanny sensation. I said 'Hello' to Rod, who greeted me, and then Emu began to look at me and arched his neck at me and rubbed his beak against my face, and then I was suddenly 'emued'. The beak latched on to my chin so hard that it hurt, while Rod was actually crying out, 'It's Barry, it's Barry! Leave him alone!' This thing on his arm dominated him. It made him a lot of money, with which he bought a big mansion in the country, and he was on every television light entertainment programme known, but he began to resent this thing acutely and would often want to appear on programmes without it. The famous incident of the *Parkinson* show where Emu savaged Michael Parkinson in a way hitherto unknown really resulted from the fact that Rod had been pleased to be asked on to the show and was quite annoyed when they said, '... but of course we want the bird' – which led to the emu's savage attack on Michael.

Spike Mullins, a great friend, worked on a TV show years ago which was a precursor of the current show *Faking It*, on which they train a punk musician to conduct a symphony orchestra, a classical cellist to be a club DJ, and so on. Spike worked on one in which an unknown comedian was to be groomed by Spike and others to be a star. We sat watching the comedian do his act and you knew there was a challenge there. When he finished his act he said to Spike, 'How do you suggest I finish?' and Spike said, 'Throw money into the audience and escape in the ensuing confusion.'

Famous stories are often attributed to various different people. One of my favourites is generally attributed to either Billy Wilder or Fred Zinnemann. It sounds like Billy Wilder to me. Even in his eighties he was still trying to sell and pitch a film and he was sitting with this young producer who said, 'Do excuse me, Mr Wilder, can you remind me what you've done?' and Billy Wilder said, 'Fair question, you go first.'

Fred Zinnemann, who had directed Audrey Hepburn in *The Nun's Story*, came over for a BAFTA awards ceremony for which I was writing the script, and it was one of the proudest nights I've ever had as a writer. I will explain. The Muppets were on, Kermit and Fozzie Bear, and I said, 'Well, I'm not writing for them,' because I was sure that Frank Oz and Jim Henson and the gang would want to do it themselves. 'No,' I was told, 'they've said they're too busy, they want a script tonight.' Princess Anne was to be there, I remember, and I wrote the script for Kermit and Fozzie which involved Fozzie getting overawed by the presence of royalty, etc., and to my amazement they did it word for word.

On my after-dinner travels I get to some interesting places, such as the Lygon Arms at Broadway in Worcestershire. It's very expensive and has display cabinets exhibiting jewellery and watches in an amazing price range. I also noticed that the whole High Street has hardly any ordinary shops, but lots of antique dealers and art galleries and goodness knows what. I did an after-dinner speech there one night and I left the next morning and soon afterwards the man who booked me rang and said, 'You'll never guess who checked in just after you'd checked out,' and I said 'Who?' and he said, 'Salman Rushdie.' It was at the time of the fatwah, when Rushdie had Special Branch protecting him, and he arrived at the hotel with two heavies, delivered some address to a gathering there, then immediately left the room and disappeared.

That reminds me of the story of the Writers' Guild Awards at the height of the Rushdie saga, when the host said to this audience of writers and directors, 'Salman Rushdie,' and he suddenly appeared, as if from nowhere, and got a standing ovation. He'd become something of a hero to other writers, and he spoke, presented an award and then disappeared, accompanied no doubt by the two heavies. Next up to present an award was John Cleese, whose opening line was 'Oh what a relief! I thought I was following Denis Norden!'

Now for a couple of memories of the comedian Dickie Henderson. I was at a lunch with him once and during it a man came over to Dickie and said, 'Oh Dickie, somebody's dropped out. Would you introduce the Four Tops for this cabaret that we're going to have?' and Dickie said, 'Sure, sure,' and then pulled a face at me as he went off to do it. So he went up on to this small stage to introduce the cabaret and all the time he was talking men came behind him with much clunking and bumping and set up four stand microphones for the act, which was very distracting for Dickie. He battled on, but the noise and the complete insensitivity of these men setting up these microphones behind him began to get to him, and he turned round and looked at them, then turned back to the audience and said, 'I wouldn't mind but it's a dog act!' He was unstoppable.

Another time I was a guest at a charity do and they had a raffle. I had never won a raffle in my life but I bought my tickets and I won first prize, a beautiful set of pewter. And when it was announced I gave a gracious wave and put it back into the raffle, to much applause – what a nice man. Dickie Henderson came up to me afterwards and said, 'Never do that.'

'What?' I said.

'Never give it back if you've won it.'

'Why not?'

'Screws it for the rest of us.'

My old friend and partner, Willie Rushton, once referred to me as a curse because so many people I had written with and worked with had shuffled off this mortal coil. Now for many years I have lived in Hatch End in Middlesex, and down the road was someone else who's gone, my friend Dennis Spooner, the writer. One day he said to me, 'Would you like to have lunch with Boris Karloff?' That's an amazing thing to say to anybody, and I said, 'Well, obviously, yes,' and a date was fixed, but Boris Karloff died in the interim and I thought, 'Well, that's a missed opportunity.' But what subsequently happened was very strange. My wife and I went to our local theatre, the Watford Palace, to see a play, and when we arrived there we found our friend Dennis King, who through his wife Astrid knew the Hollywood actress Teresa Wright, the star of *The Best Years of our Lives*. He introduced us to her, which was delightful, and she in turn introduced us to her friend Evie. It was a rainy night in Watford, and I remember that Evie was wearing a plastic rain hat. After the play we all went to the bar for drinks and I overheard Teresa Wright introducing her friend Evie to some other people and she said, 'This is Evie Karloff.' So that's the nearest I ever got to dear Boris.

Years ago I used to do a lot of travelling on sleepers between London and Newcastle, Manchester, Glasgow and Edinburgh, and one night I boarded the sleeper in Leeds and the steward was all over me. Not literally, he was just very effusive, making sure that I was all right and did I want a pot of tea or a large scotch? Anything I wanted. When I dragged myself out at Kings Cross, bleary with sleep, he bade me a very fond farewell, saying, 'An honour to meet you, Bob.' And of course he'd mistaken me for Bob Cryer the MP. Sometime later, curiously, there was a plan for me to have lunch with Bob Cryer, but sadly he died in a car crash before we could meet. I'm beginning to get very worried about this whole thing.

Frankie Howerd was someone I got to know pretty well, having done a lot of shows with him. When Bruce Forsyth left *The Generation Game*, Frank really coveted the job and rang Bill Cotton, who was then the boss of BBC Light Entertainment, and said he would audition, read, whatever. Now in my far from humble opinion he wouldn't have been a good host of *The Generation Game*. Frank was a participant, a panellist, an antagonist. He was not a host.

Anyway, he rang Bill Cotton who said, 'Interesting thought, Frank,' and put the phone down. What he actually thought was, 'Oh no, that would never work,' and Frank didn't get the job. The man who did get the job was Larry Grayson, which, because of the way Larry worked, did not go down at all well with Frank. Larry's act, involving a pianist and faces being pulled at the audience, was getting dangerously close to Frank's own act, so Larry was not his favourite. Frank lived in Edwardes Square in Kensington, and one night he and I went out to dinner at his local restaurant which was just on the corner, at the bottom of Kensington High Street, and we sat there talking, talking, swapping stories and laughing, and I thought, 'I've known him long enough,' and so I said, 'Frank, what do you think about Larry Grayson?' Oh dear, what a mistake! 'That man stole my bread and butter,' he began, and did not stop there. In fact I think Frank was justified in many ways in thinking there was a slight tinge of plagiarism in the air, but I had no idea, when asking my question in the restaurant, of the torrent I would be unleashing.

Frankie was a notoriously indiscreet man. I don't just mean conversationally, although he could be quite indiscreet in that way too. He lived in an age when if you were gay you could in fact go to prison. Frank knew no caution, he was always walking on thin ice. I first met him when I was a student at Leeds University and I went to interview him at the Empire Theatre in Leeds and the police had been round. He'd been twinkling away in the pub across from the stage door and he indiscreetly propositioned me gently as I was interviewing him, but he took rejection enormously well. Laurence Marks and Maurice Gran, who became friends of mine, visited his house in Edwardes Square once and, without wishing to – or maybe he did – he intimidated them so much that they got quite alarmed and I had to take them to a pub across the square to calm them down. Over the years many of us have compared stories of Frank's outrageousness, like the time he asked Jimmy Mulville to pass the soap, when Jimmy was standing naked in the shower and the soap was behind him on the shelf. But we all liked him, because he was such a great comic, an original. Everybody wanted to write for him, often for nothing. I mean the great maestros, like Johnny Speight, and Ray Galton and Alan Simpson – they all collaborated and wrote for him, particularly when he was having a bad time. His triumphant comeback, both at the Establishment Club and on *That Was the Week that Was*, was written for him by Johnny Speight and by Ray and Alan, who admired him so much and thought, 'This man should be back on the pinnacle he deserves.'

Johnny Speight and I wrote an hour-long special for Frank for Yorkshire Television called *Francis Howerd in Concert*. Johnny and I met up and tried to write together, but it was a disaster because we started laughing and so we had a drink instead. In the end we wrote the show together but separately, half each.

I also worked with Johnny on his very last show. This was *The Thoughts of Chairman Alf*, consisting of six half-hour shows in which Warren Mitchell as Alf Garnett pontificated to an audience. Initially I got a phone call from London Weekend Television asking whether I wanted to edit these shows. I said, 'There's no way I'm going to edit Johnny Speight's writing.' Very unlike me, turning a job down. Having thanked them for the offer, I then got a phone call from Warren Mitchell saying, 'What's all this, you turning it down?' and I said, 'Well, I don't want to edit John,' and he said, 'But he writes by the yard. It pours out of him. Come in on the show and we'll have a laugh and you can pop a couple of lines and jokes in and we'll trim it and hone it together.' So this I duly did and it was a joy. Johnny Speight's material was very edgy, controversial stuff. Princess Diana had just died, we'd had the funeral and he wrote material concerning that for Warren. My friend Ronnie Kass was at the piano, and Warren would then change the mood with an old music hall song. During rehearsals Johnny and I would go out for a smoke; I'm so pleased I worked with Johnny on his very last venture.

John had the most amazing stutter. All his life, John had parrots and mynah birds and everything and he used to tell the story about 'I-I-I-I went into this shop a-a-a-nd I saw this parrot, beautiful g-g-g-rey, grey and y-yellow job and I-I-I asked the guy how much it was and the man told me the price and I said, "Th-th-th-hat's quite tasty, can he talk?" a-a-a-nd the parrot said, "Better than you, mate!"'

That reminds me of a lovely man called Jackie Woods, known professionally as Eli Woods, who worked with Jimmy James, the comedian. Jackie was likewise afflicted with a stutter, although Roy Castle, who worked in the act, said he never stuttered on the punch line, his timing was immaculate. When Jimmy James died, Jackie was automatically out of work, but he managed to get some bookings in clubs as a solo comedian, and we were all fascinated by this, and wondered how he was managing with his stutter. It can't have been easy for him in those days, with the clang of the fruit machines and the heckling and the noise of the bar in full cry – quite a rough environment for a comic. So somebody asked Jackie how he was getting on as a single act, and he said, 'A-a-all right.' And then he was asked, 'How you manage with hecklers?' and Jackie said, 'Oh, th-th-that's fine, i-i-if they'll wait!'

Ted Ray, great old comedian, was on the David Frost show one night and he was the first guest on. Only David Frost would try to top Ted Ray before he'd even come on, and David said, 'And here, fresh from his appearance as Buttons in *Lord of the Flies*, is ... Ted Ray,' and, before the audience could laugh, Ted Ray said, 'Always looking for an opening, David.'

There were two capsule definitions of David Frost that I'll never forget. One was a sketch by Eric Idle featuring the aforementioned Ted Ray and it was 'David Frost' saying, 'And now germ warfare. Ted Ray, any thoughts?' The other wonderful moment, at which I was present, was when Eric Morecambe looked at the real David, then a serial transatlantic traveller, and said, 'Are you in New York now?'

At my advanced age I don't tend to use the F word on stage any more. This is not through any prudishness, and I know many great jokes and lines that contain the word, but I think the audience would look at me and think, 'Poor, sad old soul, he's trying to keep up with the young ones.' But there is one story that I like very much where it can't be avoided. Spike Milligan and I were at a lunch and a man approached Spike very sycophantically and said, 'May I shake hands with the greatest living Englishman?' and Spike said, 'I'm Irish. Fuck off!'

Once I was appearing on a chat show at Thames Television, and I walked into the green room before the show and there was Spike. As I entered the room he leapt to his feet and spread-eagled himself against the wall as if he was being frisked by the police and he said, 'Cryer's here, take my jokes, don't hurt me.'

I also did a nostalgia radio show with him. Cliff Michelmore was the chairman, Spike and I were on one team, and John Junkin and A.N. Other were on the other team. After introducing Spike and me Cliff then said, 'And on my right, John Junkin,' and Spike jumped to his feet and shouted, 'You mean the coffin was empty?'

I did the warm-ups for one of Spike's television series and we'd had a very stimulating dress rehearsal in the afternoon, when Spike shouted at the assembled company, 'Will you stop it! You're all fucking acting!' and I thought, 'This is going to be a good night.' I always went to the dress rehearsal to apprise myself of the scene, and that night, with an electric atmosphere in the air, we had the studio audience in. We'd done one or two sketches and the cast had all gone off to change their costumes, and I was in front of the audience telling jokes when Spike appeared. So with due deference I backed off and he grabbed the microphone from me and said to the audience, 'Van Gogh was Jewish.' So I waited. Any normal comedian would proceed, but not Spike, he just gave me the mike back and walked off, and I suppose it was a conditioned reflex – I said, 'In that case the rabbi must have had a very bad sense of direction.' I've never forgotten the death ray he gave me.

For some time my wife had been saying things like, 'If you want to build a man, use Rock Hudson as a blueprint,' and one day I let slip that he was gay, to which she retorted with scorn, 'Oh, you're always saying that, that's ludicrous.' Time went by and one night I was involved in an awards ceremony at The Palladium for the Society of Film and Television Arts (the forerunner of BAFTA). I was doing the warm-up and also wrote for the show, in which Rock Hudson was presenting one of the awards and Rock's then partner Rod McEwan was singing his song 'Jeannie'. At the end of the show my wife came to the stage door with our Irish Setter to pick me up, and just as we met who should come round the corner but Rock Hudson. My wife was absolutely alight looking at this man a few feet away from her, and Rock Hudson said to the doorkeeper George Cooper, '... George, have you got the bags?' He said, 'I have, Mr Hudson,' and turned to get them. Then round the corner came Rod McEwan in jeans and sneakers. 'Are you getting the bags?' he said, and Rock Hudson turned round and said, 'I'm getting them, I'm getting them!' I swear a tear stole out of my wife's eye.

George Burns was an idol of mine, and I had the good fortune to work with him a couple of times. George had done an act with his wife, Gracie Allen, for many years, in which he was her straight man. A typical exchange would be Gracie saying, when they were having people round to dinner that night, 'I put the salt in the pepper pot and the pepper in the salt cellar.'

'Why is that, Gracie?'

'Well, people are always getting it wrong and tonight they'll get it right!'

When Gracie died, he trained a younger woman to do the act with him, but it was never quite the same and afterwards he had a whole new career as a solo comedian. He is a rare example of someone who was half of a double act and became a great single act; Jerry Lewis is probably another exception to the rule. When I worked with George he said to me, 'I spent forty years smoking a cigar and saying to her, "And what happened then?"' – but he underestimated himself. He was a superb straight man, and a superb comedian.

George had an amazing reputation as a quiet old man, spotlessly clean and decent. On the other hand he was often seen in the company of rather beautiful young women, and it became a ritual that a young escort would be found for George wherever he appeared and performed. One day I was talking to George about this, that and the other, and the subject came up. 'There's a lot of talk,' he said. 'We used to go out for dinner in a threesome – me, the young woman and my pianist. This was a routine we had for quite a few years. And then I would excuse myself and go to bed. I got through eleven pianists!'

The subject of ghosts often crops up in our business, theatres being notorious for hauntings. Once I was at the renamed and refurbished Tyne Theatre outside Newcastle, where we were doing a show celebrating old music hall stars, and in the show was the singer Anita Harris and her husband and manager, Mike Margolis. During rehearsals Anita was on the stage singing and all the lights were up in the theatre and I looked up into the circle and saw Mike Margolis sitting there with somebody. Later I was chatting to Mike Margolis and I don't know why I said it, but I asked him, 'Who were you sitting with?' and he said, 'Where? What do you mean?' I said, 'In the circle. Who were you sitting with?' He said, 'I was alone, I wasn't with anybody,' and one of the stage crew said, 'Oh, that'll be Harry' and we said 'Harry?' and he said, 'Yes, carpenter in the theatre many years ago.' He was well known to the stage crew and this guy said, 'Harry loves rehearsals, he's often around.' We were a bit sceptical, so then we were told the whole story. Harry was a carpenter, and in the old days of the theatre they had a primitive sound effect for thunder in the wings where a cannon ball was lobbed on to a revolving drum and the resultant noise was akin to thunder. The story went that Harry was close by one night, bending down, picking something up, and the ball bounced off the revolving drum and hit him on the head and killed him and ever since then he'd been around the theatre. He had been seen by many people, apparently, and they told me that one night one of the crew dumped all his gear in a room at the theatre, locked the door and left. When he came in the next day and unlocked the room, all his gear had been rearranged very neatly. 'Oh, Harry couldn't stand mess,' they said.

Remember the Bath Butterfly? Willie Rushton and I were appearing at the Theatre Royal at Northampton, where I had a dressing-room on its own little landing, and Willie was down a few steps in another dressing-room. Before the show I was in my room and a voice muttered 'Hello, hello' outside the room and I assumed it was Willie and shouted some bawdy response and said 'Come in.' Nobody entered. I opened the door, but there was not a soul there. I could see all the way down the stairs and up to Willie's room, and Willie confirmed that he'd not come to the door. I asked around, and nobody had come to the door. Nor could anyone have left that quickly, because I could see up and down the stairs. So who was the person? We were told it was the ghost of a woman who'd died at the Theatre Royal.

The Good Old Days was an old-time music hall programme on television, that featured some amazing guests. Barney Cole, the producer, once went to The Palladium to see Bing Crosby and had a talk with him about it in his dressing-room. Bing had seen the programme and was intrigued. He said he would love to appear on it and gave Barney a verbal agreement and handshake. You can imagine the impact Crosby would have made, strolling on to *The Good Old Days,* probably with straw boater and blazer, but sadly he died on the golf course in Spain and it never happened.

A star who did do it, though, and one of the more incongruous, weird choices, was Eartha Kitt. She took it very seriously and Doreen Hermitage, a friend of ours, recorded a couple of suitably period songs which Eartha Kitt duly learned. She turned up in Leeds and was shown round this amazing little theatre, which is the oldest music hall in the country, but where the dressing-rooms are not, to put it gently, the most luxuriously appointed in the business. To be quite honest, they are small and rather tacky, and when Barney, with some misgivings, showed Eartha Kitt her dressing-room, she responded, 'This is a toilet!' Barney told me he realised at that moment that he might have a bit of a problem, but he had a sudden inspiration. 'Eartha,' he said, 'this was Charlie Chaplin's dressing-room,' and she practically welled up with tears and for the rest of the day he heard her going round saying to people, 'I've got Charlie Chaplin's dressing-room.' You've got to think on your feet.

Dame Thora Hird was a dear friend of mine and one of the funniest people I've ever met in my life. If you spoke to her on the phone she would immediately launch into something with no preamble whatsoever. I rang her one day and said, 'It's Barry,' and she immediately said, 'We've had the sex, I suppose you still want to be friends.' She was then only about 87 and at her birthday party, when she saw the table plan displayed she said, looking at me, 'Oh God, I'm not sitting next to him, am I?' and then she said, very loudly, 'If you ever tell anybody about that weekend in Grimsby I'll kill you.' And I said, 'I wasn't planning to tell anybody about the weekend in Grimsby,' and she said, 'And I paid for that, incidentally!' to which I retorted very loudly, 'Oh yes, you paid for it – money, money, money, that's you! No heart, no soul!' and we started this very loud row and people were looking at us, saying, 'Who's that awful white-haired man rowing with Dame Thora?'

On a Jasper Carrott series at the BBC somebody, not me, wrote a very funny item where there was an appeal on behalf of older people who'd lost touch with society, didn't know quite where they were and needed help. At the end of this appeal the camera pulled back to reveal that the people being talked about were judges in full wigs and gowns. It was a very funny piece, making a very good point, and somebody suggested that the ideal presenter for this would be Thora Hird. So the producers, knowing that I knew her, asked me to ring her and moot this idea, and send the script, which I duly did. Then she rang back and she said she liked the idea but she didn't really want to do it. And that was that, cheerfully agreed. But then they told me that owing to some miscalculation it was the only copy of the script, so could I ring Thora and ask her to send the script back? So I rang her and she said 'Oh God!' – she'd torn it up and thrown it in the bin. She said, 'I'll get back to you'. Later she did ring me back, and it turned out that she had painstakingly put the script together with Sellotape and sent it back, and that became the running joke in our relationship, that we would send each other letters and Christmas cards that had been carefully typed or handwritten and then torn up and restored with Sellotape.

One of the last incidents between Thora and me was at an *Oldie* magazine lunch where we spotted each other and waved. She then took the place card printed with her name and carefully wrote on it, 'What do you think of the potatoes?' and tore it up and sent it down to me. I had to reassemble it in order to read this message, and then I wrote on my own place card, 'None of your business', tore it up and sent it back. It sounds trivial but it was a cementing – ironically, as we were tearing things up – of our relationship.

What a funny woman. She advertised Churchill stairlifts, and subsequently by chance I got to meet John Stannah, of the rival Stannah stairlifts, and he said to my surprise, 'She's one of the best things that ever happened to our business, because people always say, "Ah, Thora Hird!" – who wasn't advertising our stairlifts at all.'

On the telephone, as I say, there was no preamble with Thora. Once I rang her and she said, 'Now look, look. Never mind that, look. In the act, in the act!' There was nothing before that, I had to catch up with her. She said, 'In the act, when you do the splits, when your parts touch the stage, you go "Oooh!" And the audience can hear it. It's not clever, it's not funny, it's ruining the act.' She said, 'We're going on this world tour!' You should have been with this woman, she was just amazing. 'We're going on this world tour and I don't think it's good when you do the splits, you go "Oooh!"' And I said, 'Well, maybe the band can play louder then.' She said, 'I said that! I said that at the time!' and we had this row on the phone. God! I miss her.

The triumphant relationship between Alan Bennett and Thora Hird is well known. She was superb in pieces he'd written, not least *Talking Heads: A Cream Cracker Under the Settee*. I once heard a story about a couple arriving at a dinner party and talking about what they'd seen the night before. They said, 'We went to see *The Madness of George III*,' and a woman on the other side said, 'What was that about Thora Hird?' This of course was a triumphant conjunction because Alan Bennett wrote *The Madness of George III*, so I rang Alan and told him about it. He is a silent laugher, and on the phone he'll just go 'Mmm, mmm, mmm' to you, but later I got one of his handwritten cards: 'Rehearsals have just started for *The Madness of Thora Hird*. The curtain rises to the clash of Zimmer frames.'

Alan and I swapped stories, nuggets or gobbets, as Willie Rushton used to say. When I was doing pantomime in Cambridge I was walking down a snow-drenched street and a very earnest woman scurried past me talking to a man and she said to him, 'If you see Vernon this afternoon would you point out there is no main verb in that sentence.' Of course I rang Alan and told him and he put it in his column.

I live in Hatch End in Middlesex, and Ruislip is not a million miles away, and one night I was doing an after-dinner speech and two women who were coming back to Ruislip the next morning offered me a lift, saying, 'Forget your rail ticket, come back with us to Ruislip.' On the way back they were chatting away in the car and one was talking about her husband, who was a Round Table member, and about a Round Table parade that was going to take place that very day down the High Street and how her husband had been deputed to tow a massive dragon behind his car, as part of the parade. Then the other woman said, 'Why has Bruce got lumbered with that job?' to which her friend replied, very seriously, 'He's the only Round Tabler with a tow bar.' I've never heard a more definitive Alan Bennett line, and it was repeated to him immediately. Months later I was at the BBC's rehearsal rooms in North Acton, and I was going up to the canteen to have lunch when the lift doors opened and there stood Alan Bennett, looking at me. With a completely straight face he said, 'He's the only Round Tabler with a tow bar.'

On my annual visit to the Groucho Club (I'm not a member but I think they think I am – oh well, maybe we won't print that!) I was early so they greeted me warmly and I went into the bar and there was Dan Farson. He was a well-known journalist and also had a brief burst of fame as an interviewer on television. His career was curtailed by his close relationship with the grape, if you catch my drift, but I'd always liked him and he'd originally done a documentary at a very lively pub called The Iron Bridge where they had drag acts and so on, and this became a television show called *Stars and Garters* which Dick Vosburgh and I worked on. It was created from that original documentary and the set in the studio was so good that people were always asking us, 'What pub did you do it in?' Anyway, I hadn't seen this man for many a year, and I heard this cry of 'Barry!' and there was Dan Farson. He had a bottle of champagne and so he got two glasses and popped the cork and we sat and chatted. In the middle of a sentence, one of his not mine, I hasten to add, he got up and walked out and I thought, 'He's gone to the gents.' I then looked out of the window and there he was, heading up Dean Street at great speed. The next thing I heard about Dan was that he had died. That was the last time I ever saw him and to this day I've had no idea what happened.

Something similar took place when my friend Peter Tinniswood and I were sitting in a pub one day. All of a sudden, in mid-sentence, Peter just walked out. I challenged him with this when we next met and he said, 'I realised I should have been somewhere else.' Or maybe it's a gift I have.

Although I knew Tony Hancock through his brother Roger, who is my agent, I never wrote for him. As it happens, Eric Idle and I were going to write a series for Tony when he got back from Australia, but sadly he didn't come back from Australia.

Towards the end of Tony's career he did a show at the Festival Hall which was not him at his best, one has to say – it was that great comedian in decline – and which went out on the Sunday night on the BBC. A few days later Tony was in a black cab and the driver said, 'I saw that load of crap you did on Sunday night,' to which Tony replied, 'Well, I'm not mad about the way you're driving this cab!'

In the days before traffic cones, there used to be wooden bars with red lights hanging from them to indicate hazards such as holes in the road, and on one occasion Tony drove through one of these and went down a hole in the road and came out with two black eyes. Duncan Wood, his producer at the time, told me that Tony said, 'I can't do the show on Friday with black eyes.' So they called in a nurse and a make-up lady, and they said, 'Oh yes, those eyes will be all right by Friday,' so he'd lost that excuse. But then he said, 'No, the study, the learning the lines, it's gone, I got such a jolt.' The show was to be 'The Blood Donor', one of the classic Hancock episodes, and in the end the set was littered with Tony's lines or cue-cards propped up next to cameras, etc., and if you watch 'The Blood Donor' you can see that every so often Tony is gazing into the middle distance reading his lines. After that of course he could say to himself, 'Oh, I won't have to learn the lines' – he could have his lines displayed all over the set.

At the time when Tony's career was fading and dipping he went to Australia to do a series. Then we all know what happened, and people always said, as I just did, that Tony never came back – except Willie Rushton, who always used to say, 'Oh yes, he did.' Roger Hancock rang Willie in Australia. Willie had become a friend of Tony's, and it was Willie who got the job of bringing Tony's ashes back in an Air France bag on a plane from Australia. So Willie always said, 'Oh yes, he did come back.' Willie was often going down to Australia because he had a home there near Sydney Harbour, and on this occasion he was going through 'Nothing to Declare' at Heathrow when one of the guys at Customs said, 'Spot check. What have you got in that bag, Mr Rushton?' and he said, 'Tony Hancock!' There was a terrible pause, and then Willie took out this horrible little plastic urn and that was it.

John Junkin and I, who were writing together at the time, once went to Champney's, the health farm, in Tring. I don't wish to imply that I'm a svelte sylph of a man, but it was only John who wanted to lose some weight. I didn't, rightly or wrongly, so I had a normal diet, and we worked together during the day at the health farm. One afternoon there was a great stir caused by one of the guests. I had already been told about this workaholic businessman who'd come to Champney's to 'dry out' and freshen himself up, but was unable to change his habits. He was rushing about all day, running, jogging, taking saunas and cold dips and everything, when all they wanted him to do was to relax his regime, which he seemed incapable of doing. I was around the sauna one afternoon and this man was carried past me on a stretcher – he'd had a mild heart attack. That night I was talking to a man over dinner and I said, 'Did you hear about the guy in the sauna this afternoon? This fool has been overdoing it at work and he comes here and overdoes it again and unfortunately he's paid the price.' The man looked at me and said, 'That was me.' He was now wearing a toupee and glasses. You know those moments when you want the ground to open up?

In September 2001 I had an operation, cardiac in nature and classed as major surgery, but it wasn't literally the heart, it was the aorta which was leaking and needed a repair job. I was lucky enough, although they're all superb, to be operated on by Professor Magdi Yacoub, the most famous surgeon of the day and a spokesman for his whole profession. I met him, as one does, before the operation, and found him to be a delightful man. I was a bit in awe of him, but he put me at my ease by being very down to earth and referring to surgery as plumbing. He entered my room one day with his entourage, including a senior nurse, who obviously worshipped him, understandably. And I said, 'Oh, thank God, the plumber's arrived.' He didn't mind at all, but I'll never forget the look that woman gave me. The operation was performed and I was in intensive care. My operation was on 10th September and I think most people remember what happened on the 11th, or 9/11 as it's come to be known. I was full of residual drugs and anaesthetic and God knows what, as I watched this obscene spectacle on television, with planes crashing into skyscrapers, and I didn't know what I was watching – I thought it was a film. I had no idea until my wife visited and told me, and then she says I burst into tears, but I don't remember any of this. Anyway, on a happier note, six weeks after the operation you have the post-op appointment, so I went to see the great man, and he looked at various documents and X-rays, and laid his hands on me and said I was fine, and I said, 'How's the smoking?' because he smoked a pipe. Once again, I got the death ray from his senior nurse.

There was a very large black comedian and actor called Godfrey Cambridge. American comedians often seem to adopt aggressive English names, like Rodney Dangerfield, and I love that. Godfrey Cambridge came over to record a show and, to quote Dickie Henderson, these shows were made for both England and America and they fell with a dull splash in the middle of the Atlantic. Sometimes when performers like Godfrey Cambridge came over I would be deputed to meet them and talk to them and go through their routine, suggesting various things to them, such as 'Don't say sidewalk, say pavement; say lift, not elevator,' just warning them about idioms and stuff they were saying that I thought might not click with the good burghers of Borehamwood on a Saturday evening.

Godfrey Cambridge and I went through his material, which I thought was superb. I tried to tone down the heavy American elements in it, reminding him that this was a cosy English audience. He was a marvellous comedian, but when he went on that night he absolutely died, and came off without getting a laugh, and then this great bear of a man took me in his arms and he was crying and he said, 'Don't they speak English?'

For me Richard Pryor, who is now in a wheelchair but still working, was one of the greats. One time he rehearsed his routine for us in the afternoon, and it was superb, and between the rehearsal and the evening performance, as usual, we were in the bar. Richard Pryor was there with a guy and we noticed Richard's voice getting louder and louder and suddenly he was shouting and people were looking and then he actually said, 'I'm gonna take your honky head off and stick it up your ass!' and stormed out. There was consternation, because we had to do the show that night. Then he re-appeared, and it turned out that this was a regular routine he did, and that the man was a friend of his. They are extra-terrestrials, these people. By doing that he was just psyching himself up for the evening.

Shelley Berman had a kind of 'neurotic delivery' and he drained me out in one day because I was always sent to the Savoy or wherever they were staying, and this man was just the same offstage as on. We have this horror now where your career can be ruined by the tabloids. Shelley Berman allowed a documentary unit to follow him round on a tour in America, so the viewers saw him warts and all and it did severe damage to his career. It's fascinating, but what I say is, if in doubt, leave it out. Don't let them in, and certainly don't let the cameras in. Many people have paid the price for going along with the fly-on-the-wall approach. The only ones to break the curse are the Osbournes, who became a big cult and made a lot of money by letting the cameras in and allowing the world to see Ozzy swearing and the whole family rowing and everything, but it's a dangerous game.

I've been so lucky to meet idols and giants of our profession. Bob Hope came over to do the Parkinson show and John Junkin and I wrote what must have been his five hundredth lyric for 'Thanks for the Memory' with local references and everything. Bob Hope had come over with no entourage, except for one man. John couldn't be at the recording that night, so I went front. Bob Hope and I sat and chatted. It was a very interesting period because at the time this world-famous comedian had gone out of fashion with the young ones in America. It was the aftermath of Vietnam and I remember seeing a documentary where there was a massive outdoor crowd in Washington and he was pacing up and down backstage. He was on a wobble, the money and the fame didn't mean anything any more: comedians want to get laughs, and he was very worried. Before the Parkinson show I remember him saying to me, 'What's this guy like, Parkinson?' and I said, 'He'll be doing the interview from a kneeling position.' Then I found myself actually patronising Bob Hope, saying, 'You're Bob Hope, for heaven's sake,' and he said something I'll never forget, he said, 'Yeah, world famous, but if I don't make them laugh in two minutes, they'll say, "That's the great Bob Hope, is it?"' Anyway, we talked and we chatted and then once again he was pacing up and down behind the scenery, plucking away at his breast pocket handkerchief. Then he went on and this time he didn't do the usual one-liners, but told stories from his younger days, including this one. When he was a young comic he was in a show with a man who wrestled an alligator in a tank of water. It was a very spectacular act with dramatic music, and all the other performers admired it very much. One night they were all buzzing because an agent was coming in from New York specifically to see this act with a view to booking him for a show on

Broadway, so they all wished him well and Bob Hope said he stood in the wings that night watching the act and he said it was completely listless and lifeless, and had no impact at all. The agent went back to New York without even coming round to see the man, and Bob Hope said, 'We were all very upset. We were with the man in the bar after the show and we said, "What happened to the alligator tonight?" and the man said "Tonight? The bastard died on Tuesday."' Shades of Del Monte's duck.

Every now and then you see someone who's had a humour bypass, when the lines just aren't registering. I once saw Bob Hope being interviewed in a suite at the Savoy. At one point I heard the interviewer say to him, 'It must be very interesting watching your old films on television,' and Bob Hope said, 'Yes, I keep changing channels to watch my hairline recede,' and the interviewer said, 'Really?' The look in Hope's eyes was something to behold. I also saw Mel Brooks being interviewed once, and he was shooting lines at the interviewer and they were going right over his head, and Mel had the same look on his face that Bob Hope had. He was obviously thinking, 'We've got one here,' and from nowhere he suddenly said, 'Ever made it with a fat waitress?' A moment to treasure.

Meeting the people you admire is a very strange experience. I've been lucky enough to meet a lot of my idols and idol-esses, and at a BAFTA award ceremony I met Cloris Leachman. A marvellous actress, she'd won an Oscar for her role in *The Last Picture Show*, directed by Peter Bogdanovich, and was part of the Mel Brooks repertory company, having appeared in *Young Frankenstein* and so on. When the awards were finished, people were dispersing, some going to the bar, some going home, and this woman approached me, put her arm through mine and said, 'You're my date,' and it was Cloris Leachman. I just thought, 'This is wonderful,' and we went into the bar and we sat and chatted.

The era at Elstree in the Seventies for ATV often consisted of working in shows made for the UK and America and it led to my meeting and indeed working with some of my idols, among them Jack Benny, who seemed to have invented timing, Bob Hope and Phil Silvers. During the time when I was the chairman of the old-time music hall at the Players Theatre in Charing Cross, Phil Silvers was over here. The great days had gone, and he'd recently recovered from a stroke, but from the stage I couldn't help noticing a very quiet bald man with glasses, a pullover and a sort of tweedy jacket, standing at the side by the little sandwich bar, watching. After the show this man said to me, 'Were you the MC?' and I said, 'Yes, I was,' and he said, 'My name's Phil Silvers,' and I said, 'I know it is'.

In the early Seventies my wife and I and three of our children – we subsequently had four – used to go to the isle of Capri. Our friends Dennis and Ronnie taught at Bergamot University in Milan and would have a long vacation, so they would save all their lire and then go down to Capri for a nice long summer holiday, and of course they knew the scene. Gracie Fields was still with us then and she had a place called Canzone del Mare, the Song of the Sea, with a terrace where tourists would assemble and Gracie would go round serving Brooke Bond tea from a pot and serenade them and generally do the hostess bit. There was no beach there; she had a lovely pool, but the swimming scene was in the sea, via a ladder down from some rocks. I was swimming in the sea one day and Gracie Fields surfaced from beneath, came up out of the water and I swear she was singing 'Wish Me Luck As You Wave Me Goodbye'.

One night they boarded over the pool and Paco Peña and his flamenco troupe gave a show on it. The night was utterly beautiful, with the moon reflected on the water creating a magical atmosphere. Everybody turned up, but there was no sign of the great woman herself. In the middle of all this splendour I looked up and there was Gracie, sitting on the steps of her house, in an old shirt and trousers, legs apart, chin in hands, just watching. She'd been living in Capri for over forty years and claimed not to speak Italian. We were highly suspicious of this, we thought it was a device to enable her to eavesdrop on other people. We used to see her shopping in Capri, where she never got a taxi, preferring to elbow her way on to a bus. The queue is unknown in Italy – I don't think the Italians even have a word for it.

In Anacapri they told me the story of an Englishman who fell in love with the island, as the English often do, and decided to build a house there. He engaged the services of some lawyers in Naples, but one morning he was visited by a gentleman who said, 'We can help you with the house.' 'No, no,' said the Englishman, 'it's all in hand,' and the man said, 'I don't think you understanding. We can help you with the house. The family.' The Englishman declined and the man went away. Now the Englishman had a ritual – every morning he used to set off from Anacapri on this long, winding road and walk all the way down to Capri at the bottom end of the island, and one morning he set off on his daily walk, never arrived and hasn't been seen since. Don't argue with the family.

We were in the Piazza in Capri one day and I went to get some ice creams and noticed a small man standing in front of me with a bigger, bulkier man. The little man I recognised as the film director Elia Kazan, and I don't believe in letting these opportunities go so I said 'Hello' and he said 'Hello' and we chatted and he said, 'Do you want an ice cream?' I said, 'No, no, I'm getting them in for the family.' The other man was Sam Spiegel, the legendary producer. That was the same day that I saw Graham Greene carrying a string bag containing some Brussels sprouts and other vegetables. It was amazing, the people you saw on Capri.

The venues for after-dinner speeches vary dramatically. I've spoken in caves, underground, with an amazing acoustic. I've spoken from the top of a building that was being 'topped out', i.e. finished, wearing a hard hat, with the speech nearly blown away by the wind. Once, during an event with a very rowdy albeit jolly crowd, a large man seized me and embraced me while I was still speaking and then deposited me on a woman's lap. Without, I hope, too much of a pause, I continued speaking.

I am quite proud of the fact that I've spoken to the Sherlock Holmes Society at the House of Commons. On that occasion I expected an audience consisting of people in deerstalkers and with meerschaum pipes, but it turned out to be a very jolly, extrovert crowd.

I've spoken to the William McGonagall Society on a boat in Dundee. As a salute to the great McGonagall, I thought I would not imitate his abysmal scansion and atrocious rhyme, so I did a poem in the idiom of McGonagall but in an exaggerated English voice.

I've also spoken to the Jerome K. Jerome Society, honouring the author of *Three Men in a Boat*. That reminds me that the comedy writer Bob Larby once submitted a treatment to the BBC for a new version of *Three Men in a Boat*. He received a reply that the BBC did not contemplate any more 'game shows' at the moment!

The only thing I lack to get a full house is to speak to the P.G. Wodehouse Society. Mind you, a jovial man at the Sherlock Holmes Society once asked me if I had spoken to the Wodehouses and I said, 'No I haven't.' 'Don't,' he said. 'Humourless, humourless.' The idea of a society devoted to one of the great humorists of our time having no sense of humour themselves is beyond belief.

We had some amazing guests on *The Kenny Everett Show*, including David Bowie, Bryan Ferry and Cliff Richard. One time we announced a cliff-hanger at the end of part one, and we had Cliff hanging upside down. Another time we had him made up as an old man with a beard and wrinkles and everything, and while Everett was talking he was wheeled past, between Everett and the camera, ruining the shot, and Ev said, 'Ooh, there's Cliff on the way to make-up!' Great days. When we had Bryan Ferry on the show I was given the job of directing him and Bryan said to me, 'Barry, what do I do?' and I said, 'Ignore him, languid.' He said 'Languid? Oh, the key word, I've got it,' and we did an interview on television where the interviewee never answered a question. You had to be there.

We had such good times. We had Ev and Freddie Mercury doing the Eurovision Violence

Competition, where he announced Freddie Mercury who came on and hit him and they rolled about and hit each other on the floor. It sounds so trivial, but it was quite good at the time. Everett was the Morecambe & Wise of his day: you had guests on and you made fun of them. There was an item with Kate Bush which bore an amazing similarity to a *Two Ronnies* sketch written by Ronnie Barker, based on the quiz show *Mastermind* – when Everett put questions to Kate Bush, she answered them all out of sequence. She was answering the next question. Come to think of it, it was identical to the sketch on *The Two Ronnies*, but those were great days. Rod Stewart was drenched with water, and David Bowie said to me once, on being insulted in an interview on an Everett show, 'Only for Everett.' All our guests were insulted – it was an exact parallel to Eric and Ernie.

Ray Cameron, my writing partner for *The Kenny Everett Show*, whom I miss very much, was a very ambitious man and was always full of schemes. At one point he decided that we should do a film with Ev, and we wrote a screenplay called *Suicide – The Movie*. We actually shot a test reel at Elstree with Joanna Lumley playing the heroine, but nothing ever came of this film. However, Stanley Kubrick's film, *The Shining*, was about to come out and they were going to do radio commercials for it and Kubrick apparently said he didn't want some macho voice saying 'The Shining'. He happened to hear Kenny Everett on the radio and he said, 'That's who I want. I want that lighter voice.' So Kenny was invited to tea at Kubrick's Hertfordshire mansion, and he came back absolutely ebullient, and said to Ray and me, 'Oooh, Stanley Kubrick said to me, "What are you doing at the moment?"'

And Ev said, 'I hope I'm going to do a film my chums have written.'

So Kubrick said, 'What is it? What's it called?'

'*Suicide – The Movie.*'

And Stanley Kubrick said, 'I want it!'

He was just taken by the title; obviously, he wanted to see a script. I think he was in the mood for a comedy. He never did comedy much, not since *Dr Strangelove*. So we thought, 'Oh my God, we must get this script to Stanley Kubrick.' When I say we I mean me and Kenny, because Ray said, 'He's not having it.'

I said, 'What do you mean, he's not having it?'

He said, 'Once he gets it, it'll be *his* film and not ours, and it's our baby and we'll lose it'.

I said 'Are you mad? This is Stanley Kubrick!' but Ray was adamant and the script was never sent. Stanley Kubrick probably forgot about it almost immediately, but he certainly never got a script, and that's one of the great 'if only' moments in my life: if only you could have been one of the writers of a film made by Stanley Kubrick. Ah well.

An unusual experience for me was working with the great Liz Welch – who has just left us as I write this – and Garrison Keillor, author of the Lake Wobegon books. We did two shows at the Royalty Theatre in London, one recorded for this country and one late at night, live, for America, and I'm very impressed with Garrison Keillor.

Anyway, came the Saturday, we were together for nine or ten hours, and throughout that time Garrison Keillor insisted on calling me 'Mr Cryer', and he introduced me with jokes about Leeds, where I was born, and about Yorkshire and everything – the man really did his homework. Then Liz Welch and I sat in the wings while he was on, and he did some readings from *Lake Wobegon Days*, which were warmly greeted by his faithful audience. He had a band with him, he sang, and then he virtually did stand-up comedy, with a lot of topical jokes. We couldn't believe what we were watching, and Liz Welch leaned over to me and said, 'If this guy dances I'm going home!'

The namedrops continue. I met the producer Hal Roach at the National Film Theatre when he was a hundred years old. He had been Laurel & Hardy's producer. Now the history of cinema is riddled with the stories of people who finished up broke or people who finished up extremely rich. Charles Chaplin and Harold Lloyd, both very shrewd businessmen, owned every foot of film they made and finished up very rich men indeed. I went to Leeds once to do a television programme and everybody said, 'You know who you missed yesterday?' and I said 'Who?' and was told, 'Harold Lloyd was up here yesterday.' Another of the great missed opportunities, but there we are. Back to the plot. Hal Roach, the amazing producer I met, not only had Laurel & Hardy under contract, but he had them on overlapping contracts. In other words, Stan's contract would finish in October and Ollie's would finish in January, so they could never leave at the same time. He therefore had them firmly locked in, which is why they did not finish up rich, and they had to keep working and touring well into the Fifties.

I saw them at the Leeds Empire in the mid-Fifties, when they were old and not very well, but the theatre was packed. It was like seeing the Beatles, with people queuing round the block to see these two amazing men. On they came, and Oliver Hardy just stood there with tears running down his face. I was told this happened quite regularly but it was genuine, because the great Hollywood days had gone and they were a tour de force who were forced to tour. As well as touring England they went over to Europe, where they were just mobbed wherever they went, so at least these two legends had this golden autumn of their careers.

The aforementioned Ray Allen, the ventriloquist, toured with Laurel & Hardy, and told me that he was in awe of them, as was the whole company. He thought, 'This opportunity will not happen again,' and he said to the great men, 'Could I have a signed photograph?'

'Certainly,' they said. After that a couple of days went by and he thought, 'Well. I'll leave it, I won't push the matter.' Now Ray was in a dressing-room way up under the roof, and between the shows one night he heard the thud of footsteps coming up the stairs, bomp, bomp, bomp, and he opened the door and there was Oliver Hardy. 'Ray, here's the photograph.' He wasn't summoned to their room. Oliver Hardy, not a well man, came all the way up to Ray's lofty dressing-room. I think that sums up these two men.

Not long ago I actually saw, selling for about £2.99 in a bin in a shop, *This is Your Life, Laurel and Hardy*. Now of course I bought it and I watched it and I found out later this was the second time they'd been done. It was strange to see Oliver Hardy smoking a cigarette, in the scene when they were 'caught' in a hotel room. But what struck me, very forcibly, and I did some checking on this and found it was true, was that among the parade of people who appeared on the show there were many whom they obviously didn't know. To see those two great men subjected to this ordeal was quite something.

The people I saw at the Leeds Empire in the Fifties were amazing. Among them was Larry Parks, who played Al Jolson in *The Jolson Story* and *Jolson Sings Again*, and who had been blacklisted in Hollywood. This was the tragic period when people's careers and lives were ruined because of their allegedly communist associations and the naming of names. Now Larry Parkes had named people he understood to be members of the party, and I always remember how he cried in front of the committee and said, 'Don't shame me in front of my children.' He and his wife, Betty Garrett, a wonderful comedy actress who starred with Gene Kelly and Frank Sinatra and Jules Munshin in *On the Town*, appeared at the Leeds Empire during this period and we all turned up to see them. There was a concert grand piano upstage, and at one point in the act Betty Garrett, who's quite petite, said to her husband Larry, 'That's too far upstage.' He said, 'Yeah, what are we gonna do about it?' and this quite small woman went upstage and, watched by her husband, pushed this grand piano all the way down to the front of the stage and it was just a great visual moment.

When I was a very young man in Leeds I met an old man who'd been a stage-hand at the Leeds Hippodrome. In his early years he'd been a stage-hand when the Fred Karno Company visited Leeds, and he said he still remembered the good-looking young comic, probably in his late teens, who was absolutely brilliant and played a drunk in a box who fell on to the stage, and he said the man was superb but nobody liked him, as he was very conceited. And once or twice a week he would go, 'Oh, I can't go on, the voice, the voice has gone!' That young comic was Charles Chaplin – who of course, ironically, went on to star in silent films – and his understudy, who could do everything that Charlie did, and who was liked by everybody, was Stan Laurel. That's when you wished you had a tape recorder to keep the continuity going and record this old man's reminiscences.

Frank Muir used to tell the story of walking through Leicester Square in London in a state of some distress because – how can I put this delicately? – he was bursting and it was a number two, he was desperate. And he suddenly saw the underground gents in Leicester Square and he thought 'Thank you, God' and rushed down, put the penny or whatever it was in those days in the slot, got in, locked the door and then, he said, 'The glorious relief was amazing. I felt so content and happy, suddenly I started whistling.' At that point a hand appeared over the partition next door, and then a face, and Frank said, 'I panicked, stood up with my trousers round my ankles and beat the man back with my briefcase.' The man apparently fell back saying, 'But you gave the signal!' Frank had remained bemused. 'What was I whistling? Or was it just whistling?' He never knew.

More recently a man was sitting in the gents and a voice from the next cubicle said 'Hello' and the man very guardedly said, 'Well, hello.' 'What are you doing?' said the voice. 'What do you mean, what am I doing? What is this?' and a man's face appeared over the partition from next door and said, 'Do you mind, I'm on my mobile!'

This story relating to the underground gents in Leicester Square is probably apocryphal, but I like it nonetheless. At one point there had been an attendant in there for about 25 to 30 years, and somebody conceived the idea of interviewing him for his recollections of the life he had spent in his subterranean kingdom. The interviewer was talking to him and complimenting him on how spotless the place was and then asked him whether he had seen any changes over the years. 'Oh yes,' he said, 'used to have a different class of clientele in the old days. They came, they did what they had to do and they went, and they would tip me. Now I never know what's going to happen. There's fellas coming in together, there's needles everywhere, the drunk quotient is very high, it's getting so sordid down here. If anybody comes in for a straight shit, it's like a breath of fresh air!'

While in lavatorial vein, Les Dawson had some great stories about that now defunct breed – theatrical landladies. The routine we used to follow was that we would arrive in a town on a Sunday night and go to our digs, the lodgings, and be shown round and then we would go to the theatre on the Monday to rehearse. And Les arrived at this house on a Sunday night and was shown round by the landlady, who showed him his room, and where he would have breakfast and so on. Then she said, 'Mr

Dawson, I must point out, there are two lavatories, one upstairs and one downstairs, and may I remind you downstairs is for solids.'

This leads me seamlessly to a recollection from the great old actor Bernard Miles who said, 'In the days when the chamber pot, the Jerry, as it was known, was under the bed, a landlady once said to me, "Please don't replace the chamber pot after use as the steam rusts the springs."'

My wife and I went to see a revival of *Damn Yankees* at the Adelphi Theatre. She had been in the original London production, but the big talking point in this production was that the Devil was played by Jerry Lewis, and he gave a stunning performance. Years before I'd been Lewis-proof, because all the mugging and gurning and writhing about he did rather disturbed me, it was almost medical. But as he's got older he's almost turned into a Jack Benny type, a deadpan comedian, and in *Damn Yankees* he was superb. Afterwards I rather mawkishly dropped a note in, saying how much I'd admired his performance. The production went on. There was talk of transferring to the Victoria Palace, but that never happened. Jerry Lewis went back to America, and I forgot about it. But three months later I got a letter from him. 'Dear Barry,' he wrote, 'How nice of you to take the trouble to write to me.' It was a really personalised letter, too, not just a standard reply, and that fascinated me because it reminded me of Joan Crawford, who could be hell to work with but sent thousands of Christmas cards every year to fans. You keep the fans happy.

I remember the Two Ronnies telling me they were in Montreux for the television festival and Jerry Lewis and Shirley Bassey were doing a very heavyweight cabaret and the Two Ronnies stood at the back watching. That night Jerry Lewis – even the greats can fall – had a very rough ride with the audience, it didn't go particularly well at all, and they were a bit upset by this. So they left and, as it was a nice night, they walked along the lake back to their hotel. As they were getting their keys at reception, Jerry Lewis came in with his tie loosened and everything and very courteously said, 'Good evening, gentlemen,' and they said hello and Ronnie Barker couldn't resist it, he said, 'What are you doing here, Mr Lewis?' Jerry Lewis said, 'I've just been doing a cabaret down the road with Shirley Bassey,' and Ronnie Barker said, 'How did it go?' and Jerry Lewis said, 'Fantastic!'

Television has made two attempts to bring the radio programme *Just a Minute* to the screen. I participated in one of these ventures at Pebble Mill in Birmingham and on one of the teams that day was Brian Sewell, whom I'd never met, but whose writing I admire very much indeed and whose persona and voice are just unique. One of the subjects that came up for a minute's discourse was the word 'loo.' It came to Brian Sewell, and he suddenly came out with this:

> There was a young woman from Looe,
> Who filled up her fanny with glue
> She said with a grin,
> 'They'll pay to get in,
> And they'll pay to get out of it too!'

The subsequent laugh went on and on and on, and of course that limerick never found its way on to the programme, but to have seen and heard Brian Sewell deliver that was a beautiful memory.

They sometimes say in our business 'up like a rocket, down like a stick'. The rise and fall of artists can be a sad sight.

An example of that syndrome was also someone I got to know. Simon Dee was the biggest practitioner of the chat show in his day, and the first chat show host to become a star in his own right. Many people have now either forgotten the name or remember it vaguely and don't remember how big he was – he was an enormously big star. At the height of Simon's fame the BBC's head of light entertainment Bill Cotton – he keeps cropping up in these stories – was told that Simon and his agent, the exotically named Bunny Lewis, would like to see him for a chat. They told Bill that they'd had an offer from London Weekend Television and he said, 'That's very interesting,' and they chatted and chatted and Bill said, 'Well, I tell you what. I'll give you the same as you're getting now to stay here and we'll see how much you value the BBC,' and they called his bluff and they left for London Weekend.

Unluckily for Simon, Tito Burns, the man who'd signed him to LWT, had left in the interim, so Simon arrived there without a friend in the world.

Also David Frost had his own show going there at the time and wanted first refusal on guests, which meant that Simon was starved of guests. To make things worse, one of his directors would shoot him from above, showing the top of his head while he was interviewing people, and to see the decline and fall of this former star was just amazing. A chequered non-career followed. Radio 4 employed him to do vox pop interviews in the street, but when he came back from his first assignment with an hour of tape they said, 'We only want four minutes.' He said, 'You're not touching a minute,' and that was the end of that. After that it just went downhill. He was done for non-payment of rates, and once made news by going into a shop and smashing a lavatory seat that had a picture of Marilyn Monroe on it because he thought that was sacrilegious.

Years later, Willie Rushton and I were playing at Winchester Theatre Royal, and we were sitting in the greasy spoon café opposite the theatre having sausage and chips, and a man loomed up and I thought, 'Well, it can't be the waiter.' It was Simon Dee, who greeted us most warmly and said, 'I can't get into your show.' I offered to get him a ticket, and I later spotted him laughing in the stalls, but we didn't see him after the show, he wasn't in the bar or anything. He still rings me from time to time and the occasional letter from him appears in the London

Evening Standard. I really think he ought to write his book, because the meteoric rise and fall of Simon Dee, never mind Reggie Perrin, was something to marvel at.

Show business is full of people who create monsters or have monsters created for them by other people. By that I mean creations that take them over and that they're never allowed to forget. I recently had lunch with John Cleese and his wife and Andrew Sachs and his wife. John has been trying to follow Basil Fawlty ever since, but the lovable Manuel has been a millstone round Andrew's neck. Until recently he had a very nice sideline in playing the incompetent waiter at dinners and conferences and wrecking the proceedings, but in career terms he is haunted by Manuel.

As for Bernard Manning, what can you say? One of the weirdest nights of my life was when I was invited to a charity event for old boxers at the Piccadilly Hotel in Manchester. I arrived early, went to my room, had a shower, put my suit on and went downstairs. In the bar was the lone figure of Bernard Manning. 'Hello, Barry!' he said, and we chatted and chatted. Then a priest came up to Bernard, who's known all over Manchester. He was an Irish priest, a delightful man. 'Have you met Barry?' said Bernard, and I said 'Hello, Father,' and we were chatting away and then Bernard said, 'Are you staying all night, Father, or are you just going?' And the priest said, 'No, no, Bernard, I'm here for the whole thing,' to which Bernard replied, 'Well, it's all fuck, cock, shit and bollocks, you know,' and the priest just beamed and wandered off and I thought, 'This is a bizarre night.'

On the subject of Bernard Manning, we had an extraordinary turn from him on a Kenny Everett show. I'd created this character based entirely on him called Billy Banter, a comedian of certain racist and sexist tendencies, and we had Bernard firing off joke after joke in that near-the-knuckle vein, but nothing really offensive – we wanted them to go out on the show. All the time Bernard was doing his act there was machine-gun fire, and bullet holes appeared behind him on the set. So it looked as if he was being assailed and attacked from all sides while he just carried on performing. Meanwhile, what appeared to be a stage was actually a truck. You couldn't see this on the screen, but they opened the big scene dock doors, through which they bring in and take out the scenery for a television show, and he was pulled out on the truck, still being fired at and with missiles being lobbed at him, and still talking.

Everett was a bit apprehensive about Bernard, but he was actually rather charming to Kenny and we had quite a convivial lunch at the restaurant at Thames Television. Then his driver appeared, because Bernard never did one date a day, he'd always be appearing at two different places every night, and his driver came up and said, 'Bernard, Bernard, come on, come on.' So Bernard stood up and said, 'Well, thank you very much, pleasure,' and he went to the door of the restaurant. There he turned and in a very loud voice – the restaurant was packed – said 'Everett, always thought you were a c***, but you're all right!'

Many years ago, when I was a bottom-of-the-bill comic, I worked part-time in the office of a manager named Paul Cave, and I once spoke to Marilyn Monroe, as I said earlier – p. 17, if you must know. Paul Cave was Frankie Vaughan's manager, and he also had an act called The King Brothers, who are friends of mine to this day, and a trumpeter called Murray Campbell – there was a whole gang of us. When I wasn't working I would fill in at the office, answering fan mail and so on, and it was quite a happy time really. We flew to the Theatre Royal Dublin to do what was called cine-variety. You don't find it now, but this great big theatre had a huge cinema screen and they would show a film and then the curtains would part and we'd come on and do a variety show, looking like ants in relation to the size of the images they'd just seen on the screen.

Before leaving for Dublin I'd played a small part in a film called *Heart of a Man* starring Frankie Vaughan. I would say that my role in the film was the only one in cinema history where the description of the role corresponded to its time on the screen – I played a boxing second. Having done my little scene with Frankie Vaughan and gone off to Dublin, I then got a phone call saying they wanted to do a pick-up, because there was one shot that they didn't get of me in this changing-room with Frank. Apparently there was something in the plot about it raining and you could hear the sound of the rain on the roof, and they wanted some sort of reaction from me or something. Anyway, I said, 'I'm free all next week.' They said they couldn't wait that long, and they would fly me over to Pinewood during the day and fly me back in time for the show at night just to do this particular bit. So the limousine duly arrives, I go to Dublin airport, I'm flown over, there's a limo to take me to Pinewood, I go into a studio, and the eminent Sir Herbert Wilcox, producer and director, husband of Anna Neagle, was there personally to direct me. There was one camera, and Wilcox told me what I had to do which was to look up with a puzzled expression and then hold my hand out as if to gauge whether it was raining or not. I thought, 'This is Alice in Wonderland, I don't believe what's happening.' It was done in one take lasting ten seconds at most. I looked up puzzled, held my hand out – cut! And that was it. They'd flown me back from Dublin for that. I then went to the restaurant and had lunch with Curt Jurgens, who was making a film called *Ferry to Hong Kong* with Orson Welles, and Ted Ray, who was making *Carry On Teacher*. So I had lunch with Curt Jurgens and Ted Ray, bade them farewell, and then it was limousine back to Heathrow, flight to Dublin and limousine to the theatre, where it was known that I wasn't going to get back in time to do my act, so a then friend of mine called Tony Fame had switched parts with me. I was flown back to Pinewood just for that. I still find it hard to believe.

The human memory's a strange thing, and my own private theory is that your brain doesn't discard information, it just gets shoved to the back and it lurks there in the shadows until something prompts it to come out again, as if from nowhere. I will always remember hearing Frank Muir on *My Music*, the radio quiz. Just as a joke they played a punk band to Frank and asked him, 'Who was that?' and he said, 'There's only so much room in my brain for information. I can't think of anything I want to remove to make room for that!'

That, in turn, reminds me of a school reunion dinner that I spoke at in London. I'd been at Leeds Grammar School, but I didn't join the Old Boys Association or anything and after I left Leeds in 1957 I lost touch with the school completely. Many, many years later, however, they found me and asked me to speak at the rugby club in Hallam Street in London. I had kept in touch with three guys who were down here anyway, and they were at the dinner, and there were two masters there, who'd been at the school when I was there, thirty years before. They were aged about eighty. I had thought they were quite old when I was at school, but presumably they had been no more than fifty. One of them claimed to remember me, but I think he was just being kind. But to get to my point about memory, on the back of the menu they had printed the school song in Latin, *Floreat Per Saecula, Scholae Leodiensis*, and before the meal began, someone went bang bang bang on the table and said, 'Gentlemen, the school song.' We all rose to our feet and I sang it all the way through without ever looking at the menu. I still remember from those days 'Transmitte me sursum, Caledoni'.

When I was a kid in Leeds I used to watch comics and they would tell jokes about this, that and the other, never blue in those days, except in the case of the great Max Miller who dealt in double entendre and innuendo. He'd be very mild by today's standards. They would invariably sing a song at the end of their act because (a) this signalled clearly to the audience that they'd finished and (b) it would get applause. They would have been telling jokes about anything, but the song was invariably about their mother or our wonderful country, in which case a Union Jack would be unfurled behind them. I think the idea of ending with a song may have remained in my mind as a device, because I took to ending my act with a poem – and it works. The audience know you've finished, you're not looking for laughs, if the poem is crammed with detail it shows you've done some homework, and it gives you a finish.

In 1984 I was in pantomime at the old Shaw Theatre in Euston Road. It was the year of the miners' strike, which is rather Germaine to the Greer and indeed to the premise. In the pantomime was Jill Gascoigne and a jolly time was had by all. Then one day Jill introduced us to Tony Brown of the NUM, the National Union of Mineworkers, with his little hat and his NUM badge on his lapel. The lads were outside the Shaw Theatre collecting money in their buckets, and Tony Brown said it was an apolitical situation, he was just collecting for miners' families who were having a hard time, and having recently been back home in Yorkshire I knew this to be true. So we got to know Tony. He popped in quite a lot. He was going around collecting all over the place, and he actually collared me in the pub next door and I cashed a cheque for him and one or two other people did the same, and then we had tea with him between the matinee and the evening performance and he put some books on the table and said, 'I'm not selling them but I just want you to know that they're there,' and so it went on.

I remember being with him one day in the public library, which was virtually in the foyer of the theatre, and suddenly two policemen appeared and he immediately removed his badge from his lapel and said, 'They know I'm 'ere, they know I'm 'ere.' Anyway, time went on, Jill Gascoigne put him up at her home for a while, and even bought him an old banger of a car. The day that I cashed a cheque for him in the pub he was slumped on the bar saying, 'Barry, I'm exhausted, I'm exhausted, I've just been to Nottingham.' In fact he'd been to no such place. He'd been sleeping on the floor of a friend's home. It turned out his real name was Barrington Godfrey, which sounds like an assumed name, but wasn't. He was actually an actor, and rather good at it. We found out that up north he was Barrington Godfrey – Arts for the Miners – while down south he was Tony Brown of the NUM, and he'd been working scams all over the place. He was finally caught in a car with two councillors on the way to a meeting and the police closed in on him and got him and I was called, among others, to be a witness at Southwark Crown Court in the case of Tony Brown and the NUM. Witnesses are not supposed to talk to each other, but we all met in the pub over the road and chatted away. Two guys who were fellow witnesses told me that they ran a club in the Midlands and Tony Brown had turned up one night and people were stuffing money into his pocket and he was getting very euphoric in the bar and he suddenly launched into a harangue against Neil Kinnock, the then leader of the Labour Party, and the club bouncer, a rather large man who was a bit of a Kinnock fan, invited him outside into the car park to discuss this matter. Tony made an excuse and left through the gents, climbed through the window and was never seen again. Anyway, a policeman came to my house to talk to me about Tony Brown or Barrington Godfrey and said they were keeping him in custody for his own safety because there were miners who were going to kill him because he'd been collecting money from miners up north.

I turned up at Southwark Crown Court and went in and was duly called. I remember having to say 'Tell the truth, the whole truth and nothing but the truth' – and fluffing it. You've heard it a hundred times in films on television, but when you actually have to do it … But I didn't recognise the man in the dock. He was bald-headed with horn-rimmed glasses and a rather nice suit – that was Tony Brown, a.k.a. Barrington Godfrey, who never looked at anybody, just made notes. So I gave my testimony and left, to be followed by Fred Molina, the actor, and the husband of Jill Gascoigne. He shot a look of pure venom at the man in the dock, gave his testimony, left the witness box and as he walked out shouted 'Arsehole!' at Barrington. There was much mirth in court and Fred wasn't done for contempt. This charmer, we later found out, had also been doorstepping people, pretending to collect for children with cancer, so having been regarded by some of us as something of a rogue he became contemptible. He was even alleged to have threatened Jill Gascoigne, his benefactor, and eventually he got three years. No, I won't forget Tony Brown of the NUM.

One time I was at a Lord's Taverners lunch and the after-dinner speaker, an older man with a white moustache and white hair and a very quiet demeanour, stood up to polite applause. Nobody had heard of him and they didn't know what to expect, and he said, 'I must apologise if I seem a little tired. The milkman woke me at 6.30 this morning. That's the last time I sleep with him.' I never forgot the incongruity of that. That man knew exactly what he was doing because the joke played against his appearance.

I once spent a beautiful sunny day in the company of Michael Caine and Roger Moore. The occasion was a Duke of Edinburgh's Award Scheme show which took place in Windsor Great Park in the biggest marquee I've ever seen. Harry Connick Jr was the cabaret. The late Dennis Selinger, agent to both Caine and Moore, invited my wife and me over to Cliveden, the

Astor house, to spend the day, prior to going to the marquee to do the show in the evening. Cliveden, of course, was the notorious scene of the meeting of John Profumo and Christine Keeler, and I had a swim in the Christine Keeler Memorial Pool during the day, then we had lunch with Michael Caine and Roger Moore, which was quite amazing. Michael Caine, fairly economical with conversation; Roger Moore, the epitome of charm, a lovely man. And then we drove to this massive marquee with hundreds of people in it and I was still pinching myself in astonishment that I'd actually written the lines for Michael Caine and Roger Moore to say that night. At one point Michael Caine enquired after Roger's health and wondered if he wanted to sit down. That was an extraordinary day, with these two icons of British cinema, and my mind went back to the first time I heard Steve Coogan on radio. Steve Coogan, a fine impressionist, used to be a *Spitting Image* voice, before the days of Alan Partridge and so on, and I'll always remember hearing the young Coogan on the radio. There had been a riot at Strangeways Prison in Manchester and all hell was let loose and the lads were all up on the roof, and Steve Coogan said, 'I don't understand the problem. Why didn't they send Michael Caine up to Manchester? "'Ere you, come down off there and 'ave a nice cup of tea and if you don't want to I shall start shouting for no apparent reason"' – encapsulating Michael's whole style. I thought that was brilliant.

Dennis Selinger, agent to the stars, was a great man, and he told me about something that happened when Michael Caine was filming *Sleuth!* with Laurence Olivier. Now this was a daunting prospect – facing up to the heavyweight champion – but one which Michael coped with extremely well, and they got on well and it soon became 'Call me Larry, dear'. One day they were having lunch and Laurence Olivier looked at Michael's profile and apparently said, 'You remind me of Leslie Howard,' referring to the Thirties star who'd been in *Gone with the Wind* and many other films, and Michael, just to make conversation, said, 'He was a bit of a boy, Larry, wasn't he? Laid all his leading ladies.' There was a terrible pause, after which Olivier said, calmly, 'Not Vivien Leigh.'

I'm often accused of namedropping. I'm not name-dropping, I'm just old. Judi Dench, now Dame Judi Dench – a very close personal friend – sent me letters when she was doing *Mrs Brown*, the film with Billy Connolly. She sent me a couple of letters as 'twere

Queen Victoria and I loved that. Then she did our radio show *I'm Sorry I Haven't a Clue* and we did a send-up of *What's My Line?* with the great Humphrey Lyttelton as the chairman. You had to guess what people did for a living and Judi Dench cheerfully agreed to this. It was recorded at the Almeida Theatre in Islington, and when she arrived she knew exactly what was required. She came on to enormous applause from the audience. Sandi Toksvig, who's Danish, was on the show, and the announcement was 'Dame Judi Dench', and we had to guess what she did for a living, and Sandi Toksvig started talking to her in Danish. There was no rehearsal, this wasn't prepared or anything, and Judi looked bewildered, as well she might, and then I think it was Humph or Graeme Garden who butted in and said, 'No, no, no. *Dame* Judi Dench, not *Dane* Judi Dench.' More confusion – then we got on to the dame thing and Graeme Garden said, 'Is this anything to do with pantomime?' She denied this, completely straight-faced, though you couldn't see this on radio, and I said, 'Theatre?' and she said, 'Yes,' and I said, 'Anything to do with ice cream?' and it went on from there, with this great woman playing the game to the hilt.

Often there are hidden tensions and animosities between performers. The public generally have little idea of how well people in show business get on, whether they are in a television show or appearing on the stage. Jimmy Jewel, a very good comedian who became a character actor later in his career, did a series called *Nearest and Dearest* with an amazing woman called Hylda Baker, a comedienne who also became a very good actress. In her comedy she would invariably work with a stooge partner, completely silent – Cynthia I think the name of the character was – who was a man in drag. She had about eleven or twelve Cynthias over the years who used to stand mute next to her on the stage while she harangued them. Matthew Kelly was one of the Cynthias for a while. It was all a bit creepy really, because you had to – how can I put this? – 'look after' Hylda off stage as well – it went with the job. Anyway, she finished up in this sitcom *Nearest and Dearest* with Jimmy Jewel, and love at first sight are not the words we're looking for. It was complete antipathy. It got so bad as they rehearsed and recorded the shows that they would only speak through a third person. It was 'Tell him I think this …' and 'Tell her I think that …' It really was a great strain for everybody concerned, as they literally only spoke to each other when they were acting together.

Subsequently a stage version of it was written by Vince Powell and Harry Driver, the writers of the TV show, and this opened in Blackpool. It was a traditional first night, full of landladies and the Lord Mayor and an absolutely packed house. Now Hylda was renowned for drying, i.e. forgetting her lines, the dead giveaway being that she would suddenly start saying, 'Ooh, you great girl's blouse.' So the writers were there, crossing their fingers, and in the middle of this play she was doing a scene with Jimmy Jewel and suddenly it started – 'Oooh, ooh, ooh, you great girl's blouse' – and they thought, 'She's gone, this is it, she's forgotten the lines, she's absolutely gone.' It became rather sweaty and you could almost hear a prompt coming from the wings that Hylda couldn't hear. 'Ooh, ooh, ooh, you great girl's blouse,' she was saying, and the writers were going 'Oh God!' and Jimmy Jewel walked away from her downstage, faced the audience and said, 'I'm not helping her!'

As a footnote, Hylda had a house in Blackpool where a flag would flutter when she was in residence and be removed when she wasn't, in a small-scale imitation of Buckingham Palace. I worked with her once and she arrived at the first rehearsal with two capuchin monkeys, one on either shoulder. I am not making this up.

My wife and I went to see Jeremy Hardy's show. That day the police had been demonstrating outside the House of Commons, and Jeremy said, 'They should have had miners on horseback controlling them.'

One of my memories of Jeremy was when I was having excruciating back pain which culminated in an operation, but we went on the train together up to Harrogate in Yorkshire. I still remember how solicitous he was, and how he looked after me all that day and worried about how my back was playing up. This is a rather convoluted way of getting back to the subject of my friend and partner, Willie Rushton. One day we were doing our sound check, and the pain in my back became so acute that I finished up lying on the stage being ministered to. Willie was standing there watching and he said, 'Rub lager on his back!'

The MP Greville Janner rang me and said 'Do you want to have lunch with Jackie Mason?' and I said,

'That's a ridiculous question. When is this?' and he said, 'Next Tuesday.' So I went to the House of Commons, and there on the terrace I met Jackie Mason, and he didn't even say hello. When I was introduced to him he said, 'What do you do?' and I said, 'I write,' and he said, 'What do you write?' I said, 'I write for comedians,' and there was a little flicker of interest in his eye, and he said, 'How long you been doing this?' I said, 'Over thirty years now,' and he said, 'My God, you look well!' And we went to lunch. It was an interesting table. The late Frankie Vaughan, an old friend, was there, as were Nick Vanoff, a veteran American television producer, Uri Geller and various others. With the possible exception of myself, it was a very kosher table, and Jackie Mason launched into a stream of vitriol about Israelis. 'My God, I hate Israelis! We don't need our own Nazis!' and there was a terrible atmosphere. He delighted in stirring it up and he was obviously very sincere. Uri Geller, however, had been a young soldier in the Six Days War, and he took great exception to this, but Jackie Mason said, 'Well, I'm just telling it how I feel it. I can call Barry a schmuck and I mean it, but I don't expect him to like me for it!'

Jackie was interviewed by David Frost when the O.J. Simpson trial was going on – this was in London, which is rather the point of the story – and in the middle of the interview David Frost said to

Jackie Mason, 'And Jackie, do you think O.J. is innocent?' and Jackie Mason said, 'Maybe he's innocent. Maybe he was sitting in Philadelphia.'

The story of a bizarre weekend. Two of the most famous comedians in the country, Frankie Howerd and Benny Hill, died over the same weekend. Now the story is that when the news of Howerd's death came out journalists went looking everywhere for Benny Hill, who was a contemporary, a fellow star and an old friend of Howerd. They couldn't find him. They finally contacted Benny's producer and friend Dennis Kirkland, who said, 'Well, leave him alone, he's just out of hospital, I'll give you a quote on behalf of Benny about Frankie Howerd.' So I remember reading these quotes from Benny Hill about Frankie, whom he much admired. The bizarre thing about this story was these were posthumous quotes: Benny had already died. Dennis later told me he began to get worried, as he hadn't been able to locate Benny, and he went round to the flat in which Benny lived, and acquired a ladder to go up and look through the window. There he saw Benny sitting in an armchair, watching television with a sandwich that was curling at the edges and a cold cup of tea.

Benny had died, probably at about the same time as Frank, but Benny was quoted paying tribute to his friend.

Funerals, being occasions when you shouldn't laugh, are ripe for humour. My own dear brother died in Tonbridge in Kent, and the local vicar, whom I don't think my brother had ever met but who was charming, gave an address, and all the old aunties were down from Leeds, and the wind blew and the rain was sweeping around ... a classic funeral day. The young vicar decided to embark on the Lord's Prayer, but he had a tickle in his throat and he failed to clear it with a cough, so I actually heard him say, 'In the name of the Father, the Son and the Ho, ho, ho ...'.

I once met Alan J. Lerner, the great lyricist of *My Fair Lady* to name but one, who when I met him was married to Liz Robertson, the English singer. I think she was his ninth wife or whatever, and we chatted about this and that. He told me that when *My Fair Lady* was still coming together and they were touring in America prior to Broadway he made a mental note to change one of the songs which subsequently became famous, 'On the Street Where You Live'. He had realised that an Englishman of that period would never say 'on the street', he would say 'in the street', and he said the correction got lost in the shuffle. The thing never got changed, and although the show opened on Broadway to great acclaim, he winced at references to 'On the Street Where You Live'. The other thing that worried this great wordsmith was a rhyme in the song 'Why Can't the English Learn to Speak'. He had rhymed the word 'hung' with 'mother tongue', and he said he'd had this triumphant opening night on Broadway and a big party afterwards and he was still thinking that grammatically it should have been 'hanged', not 'hung'. Then Noël Coward approached him at this party, beaming, and Alan J. Lerner thought, 'The great man's come over for a word,' and it *was* a word. Coward looked at him and said, 'Hung?'

The night of the one-armed men. This is not a Sherlock Holmes story. We do *I'm Sorry I Haven't a Clue*, our radio show, on the road. We do it in theatres all over the country and we have a good time, and one night in 2002 we were staying at an hotel outside Wolverhampton. My wife had joined me on this jaunt and we were up there on the Saturday night, prior to doing two radio shows on the Sunday. We were sitting in the bar, as you do, and a man with one arm came in. There's nothing remarkable about that, but then another man with one arm came in, and soon we were riveted because now they were coming in not only singly but in threes. And it ended up with probably about twenty men with one arm. By now you think you're dreaming or tripping or something – what is going on? Then we found out it was the one-armed golf club (I am not making this up) and I had a chat with one of them and he said, 'People say, how on earth do you play golf with one arm? Funnily enough, there's some very good golfers in the club because they have no problems with the grip. They just hold the club with one hand and they have a very smooth swing and don't worry about the balance between the two hands.' So that was very amiable. The bar was now full of one-armed men, and then somebody remarked that if they came to the show the following night, it wouldn't be very good for the applause. Then we went into the dining-room, where the one-armed men were all round one big table having their dinner, and the guy I'd been speaking to earlier came over and said, 'Barry, would you mind coming and cutting up twenty steaks?'

My wife and I are now celebrating 41 years, but for our silver wedding my wife said, 'If we don't go on the Orient Express, I shall leave you.' Willie Rushton, a constant presence in these stories, said, on hearing that we might not do the whole trip by train, 'Oh no, you go all the way there and all the way back, don't involve any planes.' My wife and I, not being great fans of flying anyway, readily agreed, and when I made the booking the woman said, 'Is this something special, a birthday, an anniversary?' I said, 'Silver wedding,' and that was that. We arrived at Victoria Station, there was a sort of portakabin terminal and we checked in, then we went down to Folkestone on an Orient Express train with salmon and champagne, which was delightful, and then we got the ferry across and we had our own VIP lounge. Our luggage had gone, but once over on the other side we boarded the train and there was our luggage in our compartment. Ordinary sleeper compartments but, oh God, there was oak panelling, flowers and a bottle of champagne, and a card that said 'Happy Silver Wedding' which I thought was a charming note. James Sherwood, the container magnate, had apparently bought the Orient Express for his wife – she was a train nut, so he bought her a train set. On the way to Venice they cheated the run in some mysterious brilliant way, so you got plenty of daylight and we had good views of the Alps, and the brilliant thing was that you were in a different dining car every night. They moved you about, with a different menu and everything, and in the bar was a piano and a pianist and we all tried to work out how they'd done this. I think they must have lowered the piano in through the roof. There was an embargo on Agatha Christie jokes, because of *Murder on the Orient Express*, but there was a very earnest American couple, to whom I couldn't help making remarks about suspects, until they looked completely bewildered. My wife would give me a death ray look and say, 'Will you stop that. Will you please stop that?'

We got all the way to Venice and then we got off the train and the whole staff lined up along another red carpet, then we got on a water taxi and you swung round the corner and there was the Grand Canal. We arrived at our hotel, spent the night there and next morning at breakfast there were gondolas bobbing outside the window. It was idyllic. That night we wandered round Venice. To our dismay, as we wandered through this wonderfully historic city, we saw a Wendy's hamburger joint and there were the American couple, for whom I'd been doing all these Agatha Christie jokes, sitting on the pavement outside. My wife glared at me, but as we walked past I leaned towards them and said, 'The pianist did it!'

Incidentally, one of the dining cars in the Orient Express was the railway compartment in which Hitler received the surrender of France, the same dining car in which the German surrender had been received in the First World War, I understand, so there was a whole lineage going back through the history of the Orient Express.

I don't believe in letting opportunities go. The tube is a fruitful field in this instance. Straps had gone, so we weren't strap-hanging but we were bar-hanging, and I realised the man next to me was Lord Longford. 'Hello,' I said. 'Hello,' he replied, and we chatted away and then we both got off the train and we went up the escalator together, talking away, and when we got to the top of the escalator he said to me, 'Where are we?' and I said, 'Oxford Circus.' He said, 'Lovely to meet you,' and got on the down escalator. Which brings me neatly to pantomime.

There's an old story about pantomime of which I'm very fond. There's this typical production with an opening scene on the village green and they're all dancing about and singing and you've no idea what's going on and upstage there's always a cottage, and there's a door and through the door is going to come the comic, be it the Dame or Idle Jack or whoever … And on this occasion there was an old comedian who was waiting behind there in full drag as Dame Trott, all ready to come on, and he collapsed and died. It was a terrible moment, and they dropped the curtain and the manager went on and said, 'Ladies, gentlemen and children, I'm terribly sorry to report that Mr Gridley, Reg Gridley, who was playing Dame Trott, has passed away,' and the audience shouted, 'Oh no he hasn't!'

Ian Wallace, the opera singer and actor, is now in his eighties, and he told me a story of when he was in a pantomime, way back in the Fifties. I must fill out the picture for you. Mrs Prestige was the mother of Yvonne Prestige, who was a little lady of limited growth who was playing the cat, a tiny little soul. Also appearing in the pantomime was a veteran of music hall called Billy Russell, now nearing the end of his career. Anyway, Ian said he was sitting chatting to Mrs Prestige in the stalls and Billy Russell appeared in the gloom, looked about, saw Ian, gave him a little wave and made his way along the row to talk to him. He gave a very pleasant nod to the woman, Mrs Prestige, then turned to Ian and said, 'Ian, I'm so hungry I could eat the fucking dwarf!'

Michael Gambon told me another story about

Billy Russell. Late in his career, like many comedians, both male and female, he became a character actor and he appeared in a show on Yorkshire Television. One day, according to Gambon, all the cast including Billy were sitting round the table ready to start the read-through and having a cup of coffee when somebody noticed that Billy had gone very quiet. His coffee was untouched, and he was just sitting in his chair. In fact he had died, and the director dismissed the cast and they all went off to the bar. This was terrible. Another actor, Charles Lamb, was contacted to shoot up to Leeds on the train. Then they reassembled and the director, who was very upset, obviously, got up to speak. 'You all know what's happened and we've got a replacement coming, so we'll just carry on without Billy,' he said, rather superfluously. And Michael Gambon said, 'A great judge of a script, Billy.'

The film *Alien*, with the tag line 'In space no one can hear you scream', was a notorious horror film with stunning special effects, including the alien bursting out of John Hurt's chest, one of the most amazing moments in cinema history, I think. What is little known, and I can now divulge, is the contribution of a dear man, sadly gone now, called Percy Edwards, who must have been about eighty at the time the film was made. I worked with Percy on *Who Do You Do?*, a show devoted to impressionists, and Percy's speciality was imitations of birds and animals – he could do the most wonderful camel. Ridley Scott, the director of *Alien*, wanted an alarming sound effect to go along with the visual effect of the alien bursting out of John Hurt's chest and although he had brilliant sound people working for him, Ridley apparently said, 'No. Percy Edwards.' They'd no idea what he was talking about, but they invited Percy along and Ridley Scott took him for lunch and described to him what the scene was: they're in a spaceship, an alien has invaded John Hurt's body, he begins heaving about in agony and then it suddenly bursts out of his chest. And Ridley said, 'I want the audience to jump out of their seats at that moment, but we've got to have a noise to go with it. What do you think?' and Percy Edwards went 'Wheee!' and Ridley Scott said, 'That's it!' No technology or anything, you've got dear old Percy in front of a microphone, one take – 'Wheee!' – and that was it! And ever afterwards, Percy Edwards would go round saying, 'I'm the alien, you know.'

They were filming *Yellowbeard*, a pirate romp written by Graham Chapman, in Mexico City. Bernard McKenna was involved in the writing, and Peter

Cook, John Cleese, Marty Feldman and a lot of mates were in it – David Bowie appeared as a cabin boy. Marty had been taken to Hollywood by Mel Brooks, and that was a dream come true for Mart, but later on sadly it turned a bit sour. Then things got really bad and he said he was coming home, but he was in *Yellowbeard* and everybody said, 'Marty's back.' It was his last day of filming, he was smoking his Gauloise in the bar and entertaining everybody as usual, and then went up to his room. The next thing that happened was that Graham Chapman, a qualified doctor, got this frantic phone call from Marty, who said 'I'm dying,' and Graham and the others rushed to his room, which was locked with Marty unable to get to the door. The door was finally forced open, and Marty was succumbing to a massive coronary and Graham said, among other things, that the management brought an oxygen cylinder which proved to be empty. It was awful. He never made it back here, and it was so sad that his Hollywood dream should end with this nightmare. He was coming back professionally, and coming home, and he didn't. Cheers, Marty.

Jimmy Perry, of *Dad's Army* fame, wrote a series

called *The Gnomes of Dulwich*, in which Terry Scott and Hugh Lloyd played two garden gnomes and all the humans were seen from the waist downwards and I was offered the part of Harold Wilson, of whom I'd done impressions on the radio quite a lot, being cheaper than Mike Yarwood. I played the voice of Wilson in the film *The Spy with a Cold Nose* by Ray Galton and Alan Simpson and I used to do it for documentary programmes and so on. So I was offered this part on television from the waist down. To make it clear who I was meant to be playing I had my right arm in shot holding a pouch and a pipe, but I wasn't made up as Harold Wilson or anything. As a result of this Joan Littlewood offered me the part of Wilson on the stage in *Mrs Wilson's Diary*, and I said, 'Joan, you're mad because there's no way I could look like him on stage. I could do the voice.' The part was eventually played by Bill Wallace, who was superb and much better than I ever would have been.

The doyen of American writers and comedians was a man called Fred Allen, who was much respected and revered by other comics. In his day there were pro-fessional clubs like the Lambs Club and the Friars

Club, where comics would meet and have dinners and they used to do what they'd call 'roasts', where they would stand up and cheerfully abuse each other. Fred Allen was regarded as the king of this environment, the absolute king.

Jack Benny was a member of one of these clubs and he was also a friend of the politician Adlai Stevenson, and he took Stevenson to one of these dinners as a guest. When the club found out that Adlai Stevenson was coming, they asked him if he'd like to speak that night, and he agreed. He then found himself surrounded by comedians, the absolute cream of the profession, all fiercely competitive. The first speaker was Fred Allen, the heavyweight champion of the time, and the roof fell in – Allen just tore the place apart with in-jokes, private jokes, everything. The man was in total command of the situation. Adlai Stevenson was supposed to be following him, and this nice, quiet man sat there at the table and listened to Fred Allen absolutely paralysing the place. Of course I've been in this situation, and the audience start looking at you with deep sympathy, thinking you've got to follow this. At last Allen sat down to enormous applause, and then Adlai Stevenson was introduced and he stood up and said, 'Good evening. Mr Allen and I were talking over dinner and we decided it would be fun to swap speeches.' Masterly.

Bernard McKenna, a fellow writer, was at one stage married to Ann Mintoff, daughter of Dom Mintoff, the Maltese politician, and Bernard remembered a visit from Archbishop Makarios. He sat down to dinner in full robes, with this massive cross hanging down the front and his hat and his huge beard and everything, and after the meal they went for a walk in some nearby woods and Archbishop Makarios challenged everybody to a standing long jump competition – I am not making this up, Bernard swore it was true. Makarios, gathering his skirts up round his knees, could leap through the air from a standing position – that is, without a run-up or anything – and, of course, beat everybody. Interesting sidelight on that controversial leader.

Another friend, Jonathan Cecil, told me he was rehearsing a play and after rehearsals he went to the pub and he said, 'I fell into conversation with two charming women, they were delightful company, and it transpired they were prostitutes, and at one point one of them said to me, "It must be awful doing a love scene with someone you don't like."' I find that very poignant.

That, in turn, reminds me of the story of the man

in a pub slagging off Wales for no apparent reason. He said, 'Only two decent things ever came out of Wales, rugby and prostitutes.' The man next to him said, 'Excuse me, my wife's Welsh,' and he said, 'What team does she play for?'

In the early days of Monty Python I was a warm-up man for the show. We were all friends, having all been writers together on *The Frost Report* and all sorts of other shows. However, after one or two recordings, when they were obviously feeling their way, I thought, 'I'm wrong for this, going on and telling jokes before the show,' because it seemed alien to the show. I was on a completely different wavelength, so I resigned and they all said, 'What's the matter?' I said, 'Nothing, I'm wrong for this.' So a guy came in who sang songs to a guitar and that worked perfectly. Previously, at the old Stonebridge Park studios, they made an independent video called *How to Irritate People*, which John Cleese said reflected the whole evening because it did go on a long time, and I was the warm-up man for that, and I think at the final count I'd been on seventeen times. I was just talking about my family, getting people in the audience to reveal details of their lives and everything, and I remember Michael Palin saying, 'You were on more than we were,' and they carried me shoulder-high to the bar afterwards. Oh, the days of warm-ups!

There's a marvellous story of a young warm-up man at Granada Television, who did an old audience participation joke, talking about astrology and horoscopes. And when he said to the audience, 'Somebody shout out your star sign and I'll give you your main characteristics,' a man shouted 'Sagittarius!' And the comic said, 'Big mouth, always wants to get in first.' So the comics were in the bar afterwards and the young producer said, 'Very good, I'd like to use you again,' and the comic said, 'Oh, thank you.' Then the producer said, 'I loved that astrology joke. How did you know someone was going to shout Sagittarius?'

A fond memory of Rushton: in the days before we all acquired these maddening mobile phones, I was on the stage door telephone at a theatre where Willie and I were appearing, before the show, doing my ritual call to my wife. At the time we didn't realise how rough Willie was feeling, but we should have done, because Willie always sat down, if possible, never stood up. Even during a show he would sit in the wings and then perhaps go to his dressing-room in the interval, but never back to his dressing-room during a show – he sat whenever he could. So I'm on the phone to my wife at the stage door and next to me, sitting back relaxing in a chair, is Willie with his hat tilted over his eyes, apparently having a nap, and I'm signing off on the phone to my wife: 'Yes, well I'll ring you later, darling, yes, I love you, I love you, yes, I'll see you my love, I'll see you, bye my darling, love you,' and I put the phone down and from under the hat the voice said, 'Now ring your wife!'

Elaine Dorgan, Willie's wife, told me that he didn't want her with him in the hospital when he was dying, even though it was only about three minutes away across the Cromwell Road, but she kept in touch by phone and when he was going to have the bypass he said, 'No, keep talking,' and he was sliding into the anaesthetic. I was deeply moved by that, as I was when she told me one of the last things he said was, 'Tell Bazza he's too old to do pantomime.'

Years ago our business was very regional. Southern comedians, be they cockney or whatever, had a very rough time up north, and vice versa. Then with the spread of television and video and everything it all broadened out, and quite right too. Scots comedians used to have a big complex about working in England. None of them ever made it. My first ever professional writing job on television was with Jimmy Logan, a man I liked very much indeed, but he had a schizophrenic attitude. He did twelve fortnightly shows over six months for the BBC and he never knew whether to wear a kilt or a dinner jacket. This sounds terribly quaint now. He said, 'If I wear a kilt the English audience lose interest immediately, and if I wear the dinner jacket the Scots say "He's sold out."' He didn't really crack it in England. Stanley Baxter, a superb comic actor, did make it in England, but he wasn't overtly a comic, he was an actor, a character player, and that was different.

The great trailblazer was Billy Connolly. I've got an audio tape at home of Bill, in his early first full flush of fame, when he played The Palladium in London and, to overstate the case, there wasn't an English face in the house and you can hardly understand him, you need a translator. I got to know him in the subsequent years and he softened his accent. He then got a booking on the Parkinson show and ever afterwards Bill said, 'Whatever Parky wants me to do, I'll be there tomorrow.' I think he's done it about eleven or twelve times now. And Parky said, 'If you want to push your ratings up you either have

Billy Connolly or Muhammad Ali.'

Billy's first appearance on the Parkinson Show has entered folklore. He told me, and he told a lot of other people, that his agent said, 'Don't tell that one particular joke,' because this was meant to be his breakthrough in England. So he came on the show with his banana boots and his funny body stocking, and the audience liked him immediately. Parky was talking to him and suddenly Billy launched into this joke about two men talking in the pub and one man said to the other, 'How's your wife?' and the other one said, 'She's dead,' and he said, 'You're joking, what are you talking about?' He said, 'No, she's dead,' and the man said, 'No, I don't believe you,' and he took him back to the block of flats he lived in and outside was a bum sticking out of the earth and the man said, 'There she is,' and the other man said, 'Good God, why did you leave her bottom sticking out?' and he said, 'Well, I have to have somewhere to park my bike.'

Now I've seen the tape of this show many times, and the laugh goes on so long they had to edit it down subsequently, and that was the one joke that made Billy Connolly in England.

As a contrast to the picture of Billy Connolly in England, when I was young my mother took me to the Empire Theatre, Leeds, at which I subsequently worked, to see Max Miller. Max's material was so innocent by today's standards, it was all double entendre and innuendo, but Max was a naughty boy. He was the thinking woman's bit of rough with his colourful suit and his white hat and saucy ways, and he always said he aimed at the women in the audience – 'If you've got the women, you've got the men' was his simple philosophy. And my mother, decent middle-class Leeds woman that she was (albeit born in Cumbria), was twinkling away like mad and I was always fascinated by that.

I was in *Expresso Bongo* and I got a booking on a show called *Midday Music Hall*. The title says it all. It was a live radio programme at midday and it was a music hall show, and I was bottom of the bill and I found myself in a dressing-room with Max Miller. I was overawed. We talked and he treated me as an equal – it was lovely, and he said, 'I can't work in ordinary clothes, son,' so he wore his full stage costume which was what we used to call plus-fours, trousers just below the knee, and the whole suit was like wallpaper. His wife, apparently, had designed it and he had the two-tone correspondent shoes; they were very flash, very vulgar, and he was topped off with a white hat. His full stage costume. So we talked and we talked and I was very touched that he treated me as an equal because I was a little squit from nowhere, bottom of the bill, and there was a rehearsal going on. The Ray Ellington Quartet were on the bill, and Max and I went up to the tea bar, just under the roof of the theatre, and I bought him two cups of tea and he had several cigarettes, and then we went back to rehearsal and he told a joke at the rehearsal. Bill Worsley was the producer who was in the box at the back, and Max told a joke about the days when buses had a conductor or conductress as well as a driver and they did the tickets. And the bus breaks down and it stands there for about ten minutes with the passengers getting restless, obviously, and finally the conductress thinks she'd better check it out and she goes down to the front of the bus and the driver's got his head under the bonnet and she says, 'Do you want a screwdriver?' and he says, 'No, we're ten minutes late already!' This sounds very innocent now, but it was a racy joke in those days and you saw Bill Worsley, the producer, bury his head in his hands behind the window of his producer's box. I was present when he said to the great Miller, 'You're not telling that joke today, are you?'

'I might, I might not, I don't know,' Miller replied and so Bill was no further on.

I always remember Max's script was written on what we used to call exercise book paper, like a book you had at school with lined paper, and all written in ballpoint pen.

So we finished the rehearsal and went to the Sherlock Holmes pub and Ray Ellington came up to

Max Miller and said, 'You're not going to tell that bus joke,' and Max Miller said, 'What, what?' and Ray Ellington put a five-pound note on the bar as a bet. Then Max opened his wallet and a moth flew out, or the Queen's picture on the note blinked, and he covered the bet, so the bet was on. We went back and we did the programme and there was an electric atmosphere. We were all on the side of the stage watching the great Miller and he got further into his act, and then he sang a song and the band played and he went off. And we all went to the pub after the show and Ray Ellington came up to Max Miller and beckoned and said, 'Fiver,' and Max Miller said, 'What? What are you talking about?'

Ray said, 'You never told that joke about the bus,' and Max Miller said, 'I was going to and they flashed that bloody light at me,' and he wouldn't pay up on the bet.

Such memories. Roy Hudd told me that when he started in our profession he was half of a double act and they were on the bill with – I won't use the adjective again – the amazing Max Miller. It was twice nightly and between the shows there was a knock on their dressing-room door and there was Max Miller, who was top of the bill, and he said, 'Are you coming for a drink, boys?' The two of them were thrilled and overawed and they went to the circle bar with Max Miller, and Roy told me they entered the bar, which was practically empty between the shows, nobody had arrived yet, and Max Miller didn't go to the bar. He walked immediately over to a table and they sat down with him and they chatted and they chatted. Eventually Roy got a bit embarrassed and said, 'What are you drinking, Mr Miller?' and he said, 'Shut up, shut up,' and Roy was even more embarrassed and that was that, an awful moment ensued. Then the customers for the second show came in and someone shouted, 'Maxie, what are you having?' He said, 'I'll have a scotch, he wants a pint of bitter and he wants …' and then he said, 'Let them buy it! It gives them a thrill.'

To balance the picture, I was in Brighton once and I was walking down Cleveland Street, one of the parallel streets that lead to the sea, and I saw a plaque on a wall saying 'Max Miller lived here' and somebody told me subsequently that Max Miller could be very kind privately. He didn't dip in his pocket unduly when there were people there, but he could be very good on the quiet. I was even told that he would go to the magistrates' court in Brighton on a Monday morning or whatever, with his collar up and a hat on, virtually unrecognised, and he would see what was going on and he would pay the fines for poor old tramps and vagrants. He owned half of Brighton, blocks of flats and goodness knows what, but he would pay the fines for poor souls who were having a bad time, and I think it's only fair to keep the record straight. Nobody knew he was doing it, but he could do it.

George Burns and Jack Benny were old friends, and George could always make Jack laugh. He was known for it, he could just look at him and make him laugh. He used to do things like tell Jack not to mention a certain topic over dinner with other people and then deliberately steer the conversation towards this topic without ever mentioning it and then just stare at Jack. Quite acute psychology. Now and again, after George's wife Gracie Allen died, they would do an act called 'George Burns and Gracie Benny', and it was an amazing sight: Jack Benny in drag, doing one of the routines that Gracie used to do with George. Jack Benny said he was in full drag walking down the steps from his dressing-room when he passed a mirror and quite fancied himself. I saw them do this act at a Royal Variety Show.

On one occasion a friend of mine acquired a press pass for me and I posed as a journalist and got into a press conference that George Burns was giving at one of the London hotels. Now Jack Benny had frequently been a victim of George's, having been set up with all sorts of situations and been made to laugh, but he was determined to get his revenge. George had come first to London and, without telling him, Jack Benny flew over and booked into another hotel. He knew George was doing a press conference that night at this other hotel and, unbeknownst to George, he was in a room just down the corridor in this hotel. Benny had arranged for a telephone to be on the press conference table, and when George was in full flow talking to journalists this phone rang and, without a pause, George Burns picked up the phone and an American woman who was helping Benny said, 'I have Mr Benny for you from Los Angeles.' Jack Benny said, 'Hello, George,' and George said, 'I told you, Jack, never interrupt me when I'm working,' and put the phone down. George Burns carried on talking, and Benny must have been fuming now. How to pursue this joke? So he walked down the corridor and he made his way into the room and he took his glasses off. He wasn't really spotted, because we were all riveted by George Burns talking, and he moved up behind George and, after waiting until he was just getting to the punch line of a story, he said, 'Hello, George,' and George Burns, without looking round, said, 'What did I just say to you on the phone?'

Here's a strange tale. I may have mentioned it, in fact I did, that Willie Rushton and I were at the London Arena doing a charity show and there were 10,000 people there and it was an amazing night. Afterwards it was still early – it had been a six o'clock show or something – and they'd given us a stretch limo to come home in and we were very embarrassed about it. We drove back into central London and, talk about timing, it was the day of the poll tax riots, and as we arrived at the junction of Tottenham Court Road and Oxford Street a rock came through the window of the car, showering broken glass everywhere. There was glass in the rim of Willie's hat and in my breast pocket. We were terrified, and I'll always remember Willie saying, 'Don't they know we agree with them?'

Sirens, smoke, sound of windows breaking, ambulances, police everywhere and Willie said, 'We're the provocation, we're the fat cats in the stretch limo.' He had put the whole picture together in his mind, and it made complete sense. He said, 'Let's get out of the car. The car is a provocation.' We got out of the car, Willie holding this rock that had come through the window, and we approached the mob, thinking,

'This is the sort of thing you see on the news, not in real life,' but we were right there in the middle of this heaving mob, and then you're reminded that mobs are just people. The mob is an animal, but within it are just people, and Willie walked towards this heaving mob with the rock and said, 'Who is the owner of this pretty thing?' and people laughed and we got talking to them, and then the police arrived with their visors on and their riot shields and batons and everything, yelling 'Get back in the fucking car!' We said, 'We don't want to,' but we were made to get back in the car and Tom, our driver, said, 'I'm sorry about this, I should have been listening to the radio, I didn't get the picture, you know.' What he did get was a bit of glass in his eye when the window shattered, so we took him to hospital.

I will never forget driving up an empty Oxford Street – it was absolutely deserted – and a young copper stopping the car. He was clearly frightened and he said to us, 'What's going on? What's going on?' It was an amazing day, and Willie said to me, after confronting that mob, 'Until just now I thought 10,000 was the biggest audience we'd ever played to.'

As I write, sadly, Denis Thatcher has just left us. I

got to know him through the Lord's Taverners – and the Lady Taverners – and he was an amazing character. His dialogue could curl your hair when you were with him, but he was a warm soul and extremely popular. The last time I saw him, which wasn't too long before he died, we were at an *Oldie* magazine lunch, and it was the time of Cherie-gate – Cherie Blair and the affair of the flats in Bristol and the conman and Carole Caplin and all that – and I thought I mustn't miss this opportunity. I was with Denis Thatcher and I said, 'What do you think of Cherie Blair and what's going on now?'

'Keep her mouth shut,' was Denis's succinct comment, which echoed what he said to Fergie, the Duchess of York, at a dinner once when she was having a very bad time with the tabloid press. It was the time of toe-sucking incidents and so on, and she said, 'Oh Denis, why do they dislike me so much?' and he made a zipping motion across his mouth and said, 'Keep your mouth shut.' Ah well. RIP, Denis.

I was working for Celador Productions, producers of *Who Wants to Be a Millionaire?*, in Long Acre in Covent Garden, and there was a pub there, now defunct, called the King's Arms. I often pass the site and mourn its passing. A wonderful mixture of people used to come in there, and one man, who I greet most warmly if he's reading this, was Tommy Wisbey, who was one of the Great Train Robbers. Not a violent man, Tommy was the wheels, the fixer, the one who got the cars, and he told me a marvellous story about Leatherslade Farm, which was the scene of their rendezvous after committing the Great Train Robbery. They were in this bedroom and they had two and a half million pounds spread all over the bed, and Tommy said they were so exultant about the success of the operation that they began to sing the Tony Bennett song 'The Good Life', and that was the end of that. Tommy also told me that years later, after many sojourns in various prisons, he was introduced to Tony Bennett in Florida, and he told Bennett the whole story about how they sang 'The Good Life' after they'd committed the Great Train Robbery, but he said it was clear that Tony Bennett didn't know anything about the Great Train Robbery and had no idea what Tommy was talking about.

I remember listening to Harry, who was the landlord of the King's Arms, and Tommy reminiscing, and thinking, if only I had a tape recorder. With all due deference to John Sullivan we might have another *Only Fools and Horses* on our hands. These two men, who'd both had very chequered careers, were reminiscing about people they'd known, and it was like an English version of *Guys and Dolls*. At one point the conversation touched upon a man called Tom the Thumb – not Tom Thumb, Tom the Thumb – and I never knew what that meant. Was he missing one or what? And I think it was Harry who said, 'Miserable bastard – wasn't he mean?' to which Tommy agreed, and then Harry said, 'I always remember once, on my birthday, he gave me a warm handshake and a homing pigeon.' Dwell on that for a moment.

One of the wittiest things I ever heard said in real life – and I was there, this is not apocryphal – was said to David Frost by Ronnie Corbett. David Frost was instrumental in Ronnie Corbett making it on television, because it was David who wanted Ronnie in *The Frost Report*, in which he appeared with Ronnie Barker and John Cleese, and after which he went from strength to strength. I was with Ronnie and David one day and David Frost said, 'Ooh, Ronnie, I'm doing a charity on the 17th, would you do a bit for me?' and Ronnie said, 'No, I can't, David, I'm sorry.' So Frost said, 'Are you working?' and he said, 'No, no.' Then David said, 'I know you, you're playing golf!' but Ronnie said, 'No, no, no. I'll be at home. It's my only day off in that period and I can't do it, David, sorry.' And then Frosty tried emotional blackmail. He said, 'I haven't exactly been a hindrance to your career, Ronnie, have I?' and Ronnie Corbett said, 'You certainly haven't, David, you've elevated me to a position from which I'm now speaking to you.'

One night I was asked to speak at the Royal Lancaster Hotel in London at an event in aid of a mental health charity, and Prince Charles and Princess Diana in 'apparently' happier days were both going to be present. I remember getting to the table a bit late with Gerald Scarfe, the cartoonist, and being rebuked because the Royals were already in. Anyway, Diana and Charles were sitting at different tables and I was informed that I would probably quite enjoy the company of my table companion, and sure enough it was Princess Diana. She was on my left, and on my right was the actress Susan George, and on her right was the actor Terence Stamp. Many years previously, when I appeared in the musical *Expresso Bongo*, we chorus boys had a dressing-room and we also had a dresser, a drama student/young actor who was filling in, during a severe bout of unemployment, and was known to us all affectionately as 'Pushy Terry.' He was a very good-looking blond guy, who was a good dresser, very efficient at looking after the shirts and the jeans and all the stuff in the show. Years after *Expresso Bongo* I was walking down Shaftesbury Avenue and I bumped into my friend Victor Spinetti, who'd been in the show with me, and he said, 'What about our dresser?' and I said, 'What are you talking about?' He said, 'Our dresser in *Expresso Bongo*,' and I said, 'What about him?' He said, 'Well, he's done quite well.' I said, 'What's he doing?' and he said, 'It's Terence Stamp.' It was and is Terence Stamp. So that night I buttoned my lip. I thought the one thing I'm not going to say to Terence Stamp is, 'You don't remember, do you?' And Terence Stamp looked at me and said, 'You don't remember, do you?' He had remembered. So this was quite a night already.

Then I chatted away to Princess Diana, whose charisma, obviously, was quite potent. She made you feel you were the only man in the world, not just the only man in the room. One of the questions she asked me seemed rather a strange one, because why would you ask it? She said, 'How did you come here tonight?' The place was full of people who'd come by car and cab and everything and I said, 'I came on the tube.' I'd come on the Central Line to Lancaster Gate, which is right next to the hotel, and she said,

'Oh, I miss the tube,' and then went on to tell me about when she worked as a nanny and she used to travel on the Victoria Line. So I said, 'Well, you could still travel on the tube,' and she said, 'Are you mad?' I said, 'No, well, you'd be a Di look-alike.' She quite liked the idea of this and we chatted on. We were talking about families and everything, and she said 'Where's your wife?' I explained that my wife Terry had 'flu, and I happened to mention her name to her, and that was that. Then I spoke and Prince Charles spoke and so on, and I went back to the table and she said to me, 'Do you want to go home?' and I said, 'Well, I can't leave before you two.' She said, 'Oh, rubbish!' and she reached under her chair and produced this obscenely large bouquet that she'd been given and said, 'Give this to Terry,' remembering the name after a couple of hours. So I crept out of the darkened room with this enormous bouquet and got on the tube and went home, a rather conspicuous object, wearing a black tie and carrying a large bouquet. When I got home Terry was sitting up in bed having a cup of coffee and I lobbed this enormous bouquet on to the bed and said, 'Di sent you these.' 'Piss off!' my wife replied.

Frankie Howerd once gave me some good advice. He said, 'If you're doing a Royal show, the nerves are contagious, the atmosphere gets to you and you start jittering. Get out of the building, but tell them where you're going.' Frank would go out into Great Marlborough Street behind The Palladium and sit in his car listening to the radio. And he followed up with these very wise words: 'It's broad daylight, and you see people moving about who neither know nor care what you're doing. They're leading a normal life and they've no idea that there's a Royal show going on inside there.' I never forgot that.

Kenny Everett was equally obsessed with getting out of the building, so if we were working at the BBC in Wood Lane, Shepherds Bush, we would depart to the Goldhawk Road and go to the Ying-Ho Chinese Restaurant. One of the things Kenny liked about the Ying-Ho was the fact that the sign on the door of the Gents' lavatory depicted a man with a top hat and cane, dancing, which Kenny thought was wonderful. We went there one night with a lot of people, and Ev had a plastic bag with him. Then in the middle of the meal he said, 'Ooh, I must have a pee,' and out of this plastic bag he took a top hat and a cane and he sang and danced all the way down the restaurant to the Gents. Now what the other customers made of it I don't know, but we knew what he meant and I've never forgotten it.

This business of doing something just for your own satisfaction reminds me of something Willie Rushton once told me. He was in a street off Times Square in New York, a deserted small street, and lying on the sidewalk was some poor old wino who was quite out of it, full out on the pavement clutching his bottle, and hurrying down the street came a classic Wall Street figure, a young guy in a Brooks Brothers suit with a fibreglass briefcase, and as he scurried along he stepped over this poor old wino and looked down and said, 'How's the campaign going?' And Willie said, 'He couldn't see me, he couldn't' – the line was done for his own satisfaction. Very strange.

During my time at the Windmill Theatre in 1957, I met a rather charming man whom most of the girls seemed to know and whose name was Stephen Ward. He was an osteopath and I got to know him, finding him to be very charming and delightful company. After a while, even with company present, he would start making mysterious remarks about his connections with MI5 and the Secret Service, which all seemed a bit unlikely. A few years later, of course, in the climate of Christine Keeler, John Profumo and

Ivanov the Russian, and all the scandal which Stephen Ward was involved in and then his apparent suicide during his trial, you looked back and thought that maybe he was telling the truth. A very strange namedrop that – I actually knew Stephen Ward.

Stephen was at the time, to put it delicately, the 'parish pimp'. He'd made connections with Baron, the photographer who organised the notorious Thursday Club, which involved all sorts of celebs of the time, and it was known that Stephen furnished parties with young women. I suppose you could say he was an upmarket pimp, although at the time I thought he was a sort of Walter Mitty character, with all his talk about MI5. Later he claimed that his contact at MI5 suddenly disappeared, and that if he rang up they would disclaim any knowledge of this man's name. The pieces fall into place and many years later you think, 'That man was probably telling the truth.'

The scene was the Albert Hall, the event was the annual conference of the Institute of Directors. There were about two thousand of them there with their Fortnum and Mason hampers on their laps for a sit-down lunch. They'd never had a cabaret or any entertainment before, but although this was the time of the alleged recession, Tony Ball, father of Michael Ball the singer, booked Willie Rushton and me to entertain them. He'd conceived the idea that we would come on unannounced, so with the lunch break started and the hubbub of conversation growing, Willie and I just wandered on to the stage muttering, wearing brown coats and with mikes clipped on, looking like two men who worked at the Albert Hall. The noise fell away, the audience were first intrigued and then had a very good time during our act. It was a bizarre day, because we followed Norman Lamont, the then Chancellor, who was booed by the Institute of Directors – Tory Chancellor booed by them, that was quite something – and we preceded F.W. de Klerk, the South African Prime Minister. At the start of our act, Norman Lamont just having been on, Willie said to me, 'Do you know who that was?' and I said, 'No.' He said, 'Norma Lamont. I thought she was dead!' Wonderful star. So we did our act and towards the end I was on the stage on my own telling jokes. F.W. de Klerk was now lurking, ready to come on. He'd already circled the building three times because he'd arrived early, surrounded by heavies, and Willie erupted on to the stage and said, 'Do you know who's on next?' and I said, 'No, no.' He said, 'Petula Klerk' and we exited singing 'Downtown'. What de Klerk made of this I've no idea.

The other bizarre element on that occasion was an address by Gerry Ratner. That was the day when he became notorious for doing a joke about a prawn sandwich and an item of Ratner jewellery, saying the prawn sandwich would last longer. This is called anti-PR, and later he had to do a whistle-stop tour apologising to his staff, and he had to apologise to his customers as well. 'We sell crap!' was virtually what he was saying. Why he did this in front of two thousand people, among whom were many journalists, is a matter for conjecture. A very intelligent man and a brilliant businessman, obviously, but his judgement was slightly awry, I feel. He denied that there had been any premeditation or malice aforethought, claiming it was just an ad lib, but Willie and I saw that joke on his autocue and someone also told us that he'd being doing it at dinners for about three years. All in all, quite an eventful day and not one that I shall forget.

One of the old speciality acts, as we used to call them, was a man called Al Carthy. I believe his son does the act now, but I remember seeing Al Carthy at the Empire Theatre, Leeds. The act began with sinister music, accompanied by very sinister lighting, and a man in a white coat walked on with a tray in front of him and on the tray was the top half of a robot. Now what was actually happening was that Al Carthy was the robot and his legs appeared to be the legs of the old man, while the top half of the old man in the white coat was a dummy. I hope you can follow the plot and keep the picture, because it was superbly done. He went behind a bench in dim lighting and then the old man came out and then there was the robot and the old man fiddled away at a board of flashing lights and everything on it, and the robot stood immobile and then suddenly the robot's eyes moved. It was a great moment, as he was there looking at the old man, and then the robot pulled a plug out of its own chest. In the second part of the act, the old man was fiddling with the board and the flashing lights and the robot stomped over in Frankenstein monster fashion and pulled the old man's head off! That was the act, and I've never heard such a stunned silence followed by such enormous applause. You don't see acts like that now, in fact you don't see quick-change acts at all, although a few years ago we went to see Arturo Brachetti, who did something similar. He came on dressed as an old artist with a smock and a white wig on, and there was paper stretched across a frame, and on this he drew a man in a top hat wearing a cape and carrying a cane, and at that moment the paper burst open and

Arturo Brachetti came through wearing a top hat and a cape and carrying a cane. At some point, when he was ducking behind a desk or something, somebody else had taken over the role of the artist. I love that sort of thing.

There was an act called Owen McGiveny whose tour de force was a compressed, truncated scene from *Oliver Twist* featuring Bill Sykes, Nancy and Fagin, with him playing all the parts. At one point he had his own little set that he toured, and he'd suddenly disappear down through a trap and just as suddenly reappear through the door as another character. What happened was that he'd have a dresser with wire-framed costumes and he'd just walk straight into them and straight back on to the stage. Nowadays it would be velcro or whatever. This was a sensational act and it was done on live television one Saturday night when the BBC used to have a music hall programme. The compere, I remember, was Bonar Colleano, the American actor who lived over here, and that night Owen McGiveny actually collapsed and died behind the scenery. Fagin went off and Bill Sykes didn't come on, and Bonar Colleano had to keep joking and talking and then the band played a number. It was rather like the awful night that Tommy Cooper died on *Live From Her Majesty's*, also on live television, when there was a terrible hiatus after Tommy collapsed and the band had to keep on playing.

When I was a young stagehand the comic Jimmy Gay was appearing in a touring review at the Leeds Empire, and he invited me into his dressing-room in which was a crate of Guinness. He gave me a Guinness and said, 'They tell me you want to be in this business.' He then devoted half an hour to telling me why I shouldn't. He spoke about the insecurity, the heartbreak and the rejection, and finally he said, 'But if you're like me, you'll take no bloody notice,' and gave me another Guinness. Jimmy Gay was a brilliant comedian. Years later he went into mental decline and finished up in Newston, a mental hospital outside Leeds. Ted Ray told me he'd visited him there and found it very distressing. Barney Colehan was another who saw him at Newston. Barney was the president of an amateur operatic society who used to do potted versions of musicals and operettas, and he said they visited this hospital and Barney was at the side watching his artists perform and noticed a man in a brocade dressing gown with a cigarette in a holder and thought, 'My God, it's Jimmy Gay.' The performance was duly completed and Barney went over, hoping that Jimmy would remember him, and said, 'Jimmy, it's Barney

Colehan,' and Jimmy Gay peered at him and said, 'I know, I know,' and then, indicating the performers with a nod of the head, he said, 'Is this part of the treatment?'

Patrick Campbell, Lord Glenavy, who appeared in the television panel game *Call My Bluff*, with Robert Robinson as chairman and Frank Muir as rival captain, was famous for his stutter. Just like Jacky Woods, Patrick Campbell very endearingly harnessed his stutter to great effect, giving a running commentary throughout the programme. When his speech seized up, he would say, 'Come on, come on,' to his own voice. The stutter also features in a completely true, apocryphal story about Paddy and Bill Cotton, who was our boss in those days. Bill popped into the studio one night and sat in the gallery to watch a recording of *Call My Bluff*, which had been running for many years, and he was a bit underwhelmed, thinking it had become a bit self-indulgent. So when the recording was finished he popped down to Paddy Campbell's dressing-room, knocked on the door and went in and said, 'Paddy, I've just been watching the show and it's been fun,' which is BBC speak for 'It's over.' He said, 'I think it's got rather indulgent through the years and it's become the you and Frank Muir show and it's lost its edge and its spark and I really think after this series – and you know it's been marvellous what you've done – but I think after this series, we'll probably call it a day.' And Paddy Campbell said, 'C-c-c-c-come in!'

Together with Marty Feldman and a whole gang of people I was sitting in a bar, a fairly constant scenario in these stories, at London Weekend Television, where they used to have a tannoy system for calling people to Reception. The BBC had the same thing, and of course people used to put out joke calls for 'Mr Andrew Pandy' and other such witticisms, and we were just sitting there when the voice on the tannoy said – and it was the corniest show business name you can imagine – 'Gloria Lamarr to Reception, please,' and Marty Feldman gave a great sigh and got up and walked out. The timing was impeccable.

I got a phone call one day offering me an after-dinner speaking job in Houston, Texas. I honestly misheard this on the phone and thought, 'Was the guy referring to Euston? Euston Station? A hotel in Euston? What?' Then he said 'Texas' and sure enough it was Texas – The British American Business Association – and Caledonian Airlines were still operating there. They flew direct to Houston, and although I'm not the greatest fan of flying, nonetheless I flew out to speak to these massed ranks of Texans and Brits and had a wonderful time. Gauging it carefully, I didn't do the parochial stuff because the Texans would have been baffled, quite understandably, but I tried to do a mix of straight one-liners and jokes that would travel, plus some nonsense for the Brits. While I was there I met a journalist called Ewing (which must be a local name when one remembers *Dallas*) and I was looked after by a man called Roger Luxton, a Kenneth Moore clone if ever there was one. He was a lovely man and I had a very good night. I remember saying, as the wine went down, that Margaret Thatcher seemed much more popular there than she did back home. This went down like the proverbial … The Texans didn't like me for that and the Brits liked me even less.

I wasn't flying back until the Sunday night, so the next day we went sailing in Galveston Bay with a very jolly extrovert guy who sang old, dirty nautical songs and a happy haze ensued. I looked up at one point and I couldn't see the sky – we were in a shipping lane and were right next to a tanker. I flew home, arriving midday our time, went into my local pub and a guy said, 'I didn't see you at the weekend. Did you have your feet up?' and I said, 'Yes, 30,000 feet.'

I have, on more than one occasion, been asked, as a sort of ersatz Michael Aspel or Eamonn Andrews, to burst into a restaurant and confront an amazed man or woman with a red book and then proceed with *This Is Your Life*. I did it once in a restaurant that had two rooms, and I burst into the wrong room to the astonishment of all concerned. They asked me to stay for a drink but I had to move on to the right room.

My acquaintanceship with *This Is Your Life* has lasted many years and I think I'm a friend of the family now. I only ever appeared when I was genuinely a friend and/or colleague of the subject of the programme. I actually turned down one or two because I didn't want to look as though I just wanted to be on television – that is, when I didn't really know the person concerned – because that's painfully apparent on that programme.

I have many fond memories of *This Is Your Life*. One was sitting in the stalls with Bob Todd, the legendary bald man from the Benny Hill show who I worked with a lot, when we'd both been invited to the show, and I knew for certain it was *him* but they'd told him it was me, which was a very strange sensation. It transpired that this comic actor, a former farmer and no stranger to the grape, to put it delicately, had been something of a hero during the war – not that he'd ever told us. He'd landed a burning plane. That was an amazing day.

Earlier I'd done one with Pam Ayres, back in the days when Eamonn Andrews was presenting. He mentioned her very first boyfriend and then there was the burst of music and we heard the voice, and sure enough they'd found him in America and they'd flown him over. On he came and he embraced Pam, and she burst into tears and the audience were very moved. At the drinks party afterwards she said, 'They were tears of rage. I never wanted to see him again!'

Bernard Cribbins was done by *This Is Your Life* years ago, and my wife and I were invited to be in the audience. Old friend that I was, I wasn't invited to be on the programme, and at the drinks afterwards Eamonn Andrews told me, very cheerfully, that I was now barred. I think I'd equalled Lionel Blair's record or something – I'd been on eight or nine times – and

Eamonn said, 'The mention of your name got a laugh at the meeting.'

Tommy Steele told the story of being invited somewhere under some pretext. They were really gulling him into doing *This Is Your Life*, but as he walked down the street to which he was being lured, a whole coach went past him with his life in it and he thought he was having a fantasy.

I realised, to my dismay, what a good liar my wife Terry was when I came home one day and there was a piece of paper by the phone with a phone number on it and the words 'This Is Your Life'. One of our dogs had crapped on the stairs, so I went away to attend to that and when I came back the piece of paper had gone, so I challenged Terry about this, saying, 'What was that all about?' and without a pause she said, 'Oh, they rang up about a *This Is Your Life* but they said don't worry, it's gone away, you're not needed.'

There are moments in *This Is Your Life* which are like an out of body experience, as if it's happening to somebody else. I couldn't help noticing on mine that there was a piano there and on top of the piano was a trumpet, and while I was concentrating on the show, obviously, and greeting the guests and talking to Michael Aspel, I couldn't take my eyes off this piano with the trumpet on top of it and, sure enough, my old friend Colin Sell came on. We'd known each other for some years through *I'm Sorry I Haven't a Clue* and he and I tour all the time doing a theatre show called *The First Farewell Tour*. Then Colin suddenly announced, without consulting me, that I was going to sing 'Show Me the Way to Go Home', and Humphrey Lyttelton appeared and was hilarious, and then I did sing 'Show Me the Way to Go Home' accompanied by Colin Sell at the piano and Humphrey Lyttelton playing obligato on trumpet. These are golden moments. You can't substitute anything for those.

I must be utterly memorable. Among my fellow performers in the show *Expresso Bongo* in 1958 in London were Charles Gray, making one of his first major appearances in the West End before going on to film fame, and a wonderful Jewish actor called Meier Tzelniker, who played the agent and had two of the best songs in the show. Many years later I went into a pub called The Coffee House in Beak Street in Soho, and saw a lone figure sitting on a stool reading a paper. It was Charles Gray, and I hadn't seen him for years. 'Barry,' he said, and we embraced and we chatted and we talked and talked and talked, then he looked at his watch and said, 'I have to go, my dear.

Lovely to see you again, Tookie.' That's how memorable I am. Then later I met the aforementioned Meier Tzelniker on a train going to Hampton Wick, of all places, and he, like Charles, beamed and we embraced and talked and talked and talked, and we got off at the same station, Hampton Wick. As we parted on the pavement he said, 'Whatever happened to that fellow Cryer?'

This went on and on. At the end of the first Comic Relief there was a small, intimate soirée for people who'd worked on the show, and Princess Anne came, and was introduced to all of us there. I was talking to Jimmy Mulville and Rory McGrath, and Paul, this friend of mine, introduced me to the Princess, saying, 'And this is Barry Took,' and I thought this isn't the moment, and I said, 'Hello, hello', and the moment passed, not important. About three weeks later, my wife and I were at a do at the Café Royal in London and there was Princess Anne again, and there was this long line of people waiting to be introduced, but the man doing the introductions this time had an immaculate memory, he remembered everybody's name, and when they got to ours he said, 'This is Mr and Mrs Barry Cryer,' and she said, 'You were Barry Took last time.'

I always used to share these things with Tookie and we would swap stories, because the same thing used to happen to Barry all the time. He was once referred to as Barry Cryer on *Just a Minute*. The game went on all through the years, but one day he rang me and he said, 'I win.' I said, 'What are you talking about, I win?' He said he had been with Princess Anne the previous night, and she had said to him, 'Is there someone called Barry Cryer?' and he said, 'Yes, an old friend of mine,' and she said, 'Well, can we have a do where both you buggers are there and I can sort out which is which?'

Not long before Barry died he managed a day of golf and a man came up to Barry at the golf club and said, 'Ah, Mr Cryer,' and Barry said 'Not again!' I went to Barry's funeral, as I told all our mutual friends, just to remove any remaining confusion.

Looking back, there are so many memories. Jimmy Edwards and I were both born on the same day, though not in the same year. So we were, in a sense, twins. Both Jimmy and Frankie Howerd were gay, as I touched on earlier, and it was another age, another era, so they were haunted, hunted men – you could go to prison. They also drank a lot – I'm not being a hypocrite, I like a drink, but they were tortured souls. I was very fond of both of them.

Jimmy and I were once getting on a breakfast train

to Leeds, the 7.55 from Kings Cross, and it was our birthday, 23 March, and Jimmy bellowed at me, 'It's our birthday!' and I said, 'I know, I know,' and he said, 'Champagne after breakfast,' and I said, 'Great Jim, thank you very much,' and the steward was hovering, because he'd spotted Jimmy Edwards. Jimmy ordered the champagne and we had our bacon and eggs and the steward was hovering all the time.

There was another star comedian in those days, of course, called Jimmy Wheeler, who was a cockney comedian, and after Jimmy Edwards and I finished our breakfast, the steward came up and said, 'The champagne's ready, any time you want it, Mr Wheeler,' to which Jimmy replied, 'That's ruined my fucking birthday!'

Another time we were in Leeds for a Variety Club lunch. I left the train and went off to the Queens Hotel, bang next door to the station, to join the merry band and have a drink before lunch, and the great Edwards had disappeared and I thought, 'Where's he gone?' An hour or so later he reappeared in very good shape and I thought, 'Where did you go? Where have you been? What have you been doing?' Anyway, we sat down at this Variety Club lunch and at our table was a show business vicar. Let me elucidate. He was a guy who loved show business and he had a dog collar on and he was very excited at being with the showbiz folk – he was like a groupie.

Jimmy gave him a beady glare and then I was asked up to speak and I went up and did my piece. Afterwards I returned to the table and sat down and Jimmy Edwards was announced. He came up and looked at the audience and said, 'We've got a fucking vicar at our table! God, I hate organised religion!' You can imagine the frisson. I love these characters – I met them, I knew them, I lived with them.

I went to Jimmy's funeral with Peter Charlesworth, his agent, and Peter told me one or two stories. He said he'd acquired a relationship with a local police sergeant, in Sussex where Jimmy lived, and Jimmy would misbehave and drink a lot and the local police sergeant would ring Peter and say, 'We've got Mr Edwards again.' One night the police sergeant rang and said, 'Hello, Mr Charlesworth, we've got Mr Edwards again,' and Peter said, 'Oh, what is it now?' and the sergeant said, 'No, no, it's all right. He was singing selections from *La Traviata* in the street,' and Peter said, 'Oh dear,' and the sergeant said, 'Don't worry, I put my coat on over the dress and we took him home.' Now there's a thought.

I was standing up on the tube one day and I noticed there was a man sitting holding his ticket in his hand in a very touristy way and I thought, 'That's Willy Russell,' the writer of *Blood Brothers, Shirley Valentine* and so on. The seat next to him became vacant and I went and sat there and he said, 'Barry Cryer,' and I said, 'Yes. Willy Russell.'

'I thought it was you,' he said, 'but I thought that c*** would never be on the tube!' These are moving meetings.

Then later I found myself sitting next to Ken Russell, and he told me about his new film, *The Lair of the White Worm*. You never know who you're going to meet on the tube.

A few years ago I was making my way on the Jubilee Line to the Savoy Theatre to do a charity show, and the train was just crawling along. The man next to me was reading a paper and being very English and not looking up when suddenly the train gave an enormous lurch and I, involuntarily, said to him 'What was that?' No reply whatsoever, and we crawled into Green Park station very, very slowly and then the doors flew open and guys ran in with guns and flak jackets and poised themselves, aiming through the connecting doors of the compartment. The armed man standing next to me with his gun said, quite politely, 'Do excuse me,' and leaned on the arm of the seat pointing his gun, and of course the compartment was frozen – we thought, 'What is this?' Then a policeman with a checkered hat entered holding up a small revolver. He walked down the compartment and said, 'When I pass you, get out of the door quick!' By now it was becoming totally unreal, and he walked past me so I went out of the door like a bat out of hell and headed for the exit. I got on to the escalator and there was my companion of just before who'd gone on reading his paper when I said 'What was that?' when the train lurched, and now on the escalator he looked at me and said, 'Hence the lurch!' – which I thought was succinct and so accurate. That night there was nothing about it in the evening papers, and nothing on television either. This was during the so-called ceasefire in Northern Ireland, regarding which somebody said to me, 'Ceasefire being translated means reload.' It may have been an exercise, but we'll never know.

Not long afterwards my wife was at Maida Vale tube station waiting for the train and a similar thing happened. Guys in flak jackets and carrying guns clattered down the stairway, and as the train came in they joined the passengers and the same routine ensued. To this day, I've never discovered what was going on.

I travel on trains a lot, not being a driver, and despite all the vicissitudes of privatisation it is still my favourite form of travel. One day I was having a conversation about trains and railways with my friend

Howard Eldridge, a jovial drinking companion at my local pub, a sound man par excellence and a theatre technician of vast experience. Howard and I began to talk about the great Isambard Kingdom Brunel, and Howard said to me, 'Do you know that out of Temple Meads Station at Bristol there is a quite long tunnel?' and I said 'Yes', and he said, 'Do you know that one day every year, just one day, the sun shines down that tunnel?' and I said 'Yes', and he said, 'That is Brunel's birthday.' Then I said, 'What happens if the sun isn't shining that day?' and he said, 'Don't ruin the story.' Brunel had apparently calculated the trajectory and everything. You be the judge.

When I was growing up in Leeds our neighbours, the Taskers, were regarded as rather affluent, and once they had a children's party for their son Dean. I was present at the party, where they had a semi-professional ventriloquist entertaining us, and that was when I first became interested in ventriloquists. I talked to him afterwards and he was staying over-night with them before going on somewhere else the next day, and I asked if his doll could stay with me that night, to which he agreed. I was thrilled by this, and before going to sleep I put the doll on the chair next to my bed. I remember the doll was staring straight at me and this began to give me the creeps, so I turned its head round so it was facing away. I then went to sleep, but I woke up during the night and the moonlight was coming in through the window and the doll was looking at me again. All that had happened obviously was that the angle at which it was seated in the chair had caused its head to swing back, but I never forgot that.

I've worked with many ventriloquists over the years. When I first came into the profession and was doing variety, I shared a dressing-room with a young vent called Skinner, and I was absolutely fascinated with the doll. They used to talk to each other on the stairs on their way to and from the stage. One night during the interval he put a towel over the doll's head and popped out of the dressing-room, leaving the doll sitting on a chair. I would never do it now, but I was new to the business and pretty green in those days, and I was fascinated by the workings of the doll. So I took the towel off its head, looked through the hole in the back and saw the pole the head was on and the bit that you operated with your thumb and so on, and as I was looking the vent came back into the room. 'Leave him alone, he's resting,' he said. I never forgot that, and for the rest of that week whenever I heard him talking to the doll on the stairs and arguing about something that had happened in the act, a frisson crept over me.

There was a brilliant ventriloquist called Dennis Spicer who sadly was killed in a car crash. In the wreckage the police found a pair of small shoes and they assumed there must have been a child in the car, but that was not the case – they were the doll's shoes that had been ripped off in the crash.

Once I was in Newcastle doing a show with Ted Ray and others at Tyne Tees Television, and Dennis, who was also appearing, arrived very late. He finally entered the dressing-room, apologising profusely and talking about the traffic, and put a case down on the table. He opened the case, took out a small doll and hung it on a hook on the wall. Then he said, 'I must have a pee, I must have a cup of tea, I'll be back in a minute, sorry about all this,' and left the room. He'd left the case unfastened, and the lid was ajar, so Ted Ray said, 'Oh, let's have a look' and he opened the lid of the case, and there was a frog with rolling eyes and all sorts of interesting props and bits and pieces in there, and then Ted said, 'We shouldn't be doing this.' He closed the lid, and when Dennis Spicer entered the room the doll on the wall said, 'He's had a look in your case, Dennis.'

I saw Dennis Spicer do *Sunday Night at The London Palladium* and it was a stunningly accomplished act. But there was one fairly ordinary bit in it where a battered-looking doll is sitting on a chair.

And Dennis got this rather unexciting, old-fashioned doll to recite the alphabet while he, Dennis, was drinking a glass of water, and when that bit was over I thought, 'Well, that's less than your best.' I didn't think it was very impressive. At the end of his act he took his bow and went offstage and the audience kept applauding, so he came back on and whistled and the doll got off the chair and ran towards him and took a bow with him and they went off together. It was amazing. Dennis got the idea from the film *Dead of Night*, which every ventriloquist must have seen. It's a portmanteau film with several stories, and one of them features Michael Redgrave as a ventriloquist whose doll takes him over, and at one point he tries to shut the doll up by putting his hand over its mouth and it bites him. And at the end, when he's completely hallucinating, he's talking with the doll's voice and the doll comes out of the chair and comes towards him. This was a small actor heavily made up, which is where Dennis got the idea.

Terri Rogers was a brilliant ventriloquist, but she was a sex-change ventriloquist – she had been a man. A sex-change ventriloquist, how much more do you need? Terri and I worked together in Lisburn, outside Belfast, during the heavy times, at the Conway Hotel which had been blown up previously, and was now surrounded by wire fencing. You were shown into a shed as you arrived. There was a luggage search, a body search and then we went in and I thought, 'I wonder what the score is tonight?' and on the table in reception I saw a brochure with a big glossy picture of Ian Paisley on the front. 'I think I've got the picture,' I said to myself. That night I did the after-dinner speech and Terri came on later to do the cabaret, but in the middle of her act the manager came on and whispered to her, and she announced that we had to evacuate the building owing to a bomb scare. Both Terri and I thought, 'We're English, we're taking this very seriously, we'll get out,' and we went down with the customers and the band. We went to a lodge in the hotel grounds and told each other stories and sang songs and recited limericks, and then we were told we could go back in and the manager said to Terri, 'You don't have to go on again, you've done yours.' But Terri said, 'No, I was only half-way through the act, I'll do the rest of it,' and the manager said, 'That's great, thank you very much.' So Terri went back on with her doll to enormous applause, and the doll looked straight at the audience and said 'What the fuck was that?'

Arthur Worsley was a ventriloquist who never spoke a word on stage, the doll did the whole act, but later in his career Arthur would suddenly come out with just one word. The doll would say something and Arthur would say 'No' and it was incredible to see the doll's reaction, the way its head would swivel off with amazement at this man, who'd never spoken for years, suddenly saying one word. I was the chairman of a TV show called *Jokers Wild*, where six comics vied with each other telling jokes, and we had Arthur Worsley and his doll on one week and it was quite uncanny. There was a moment at the end of the first half of the show where a comedian would have to mount a small rostrum and tell jokes to the audience for one minute and we would log how many laughs he got in that statutory minute. So Arthur was up there with the doll and they were about half-way through when the doll leaned back over Arthur's shoulder and said, 'How long have we got, Barry?' and I actually leaned over so I could speak to him, so complete was the illusion.

The art goes on, and David Strassman, a brilliant American, has an evil doll called Chuckie whose eyes glow in the dark and who spits at the front row. It's only water, but you should see the people jump, and the doll gives great force to such charming lines as 'Is this where I go into the audience and kill somebody?' but the tour de force is when he has a row with this doll, and walks off the stage leaving the doll sitting alone on the stool. Suddenly its eyes move, looking off stage to where he's gone, and the doll says, 'Has he gone?' It's just an amazing moment. This is all done by computer technology, and the climax of the act is four stegosauruses, conducted by David, singing 'Bohemian Rhapsody'. These people are just astonishing.

The tradition also continues with Nina Conti, daughter of Tom Conti, the actor. She doesn't use a doll, but a glove puppet, a monkey, on the end of her arm. She can contort the face into all sorts of expressions, and she is unique among the ventriloquists that I've heard in that her puppet has a voice that is completely different from hers in timbre and range. It is just amazing, it is a separate entity.

The permutations are endless. I once saw a woman ventriloquist who was topless. I never saw her lips move!

This is a visual story, so I hope you get the picture. Making my way over the bridge in Hatch End to my pub, The Moon, I approached the bus stop at the foot of the bridge. Standing at the bus stop was a Japanese guy looking anxiously for the bus. It was approaching. You couldn't reproduce this timing. Jacques Tati would have killed for this, because as I was just about to pass the Japanese guy he stuck his hand out to hail the approaching bus and punched me in the face. He was prostrate with apologies and nearly missed the bus.

This year, I was rung up and asked if I would like to work on a stage show for Jackie Mason, a sort of revival of *Hellzapoppin'* with Jackie as the compere, introducing the acts which would be coming on, and doing his own spot at the end of the show. Once again, I agreed with alacrity and I also got my dear old friend Dick Vosburgh involved. I thought, if ever a man was meant to write for Jackie Mason, it's Dick Vosburgh, who is one of the funniest men around. He's also a brilliant lyricist. A year or two ago I did a show written by Dick called *The Saint She Ain't*, in which I played a sort of W.C. Fields character. Dick and I were duly co-opted. You had to ring Jackie at the most extraordinary times, or he would ring you, because he was in New York and obviously because of the time difference you would get calls at the most ridiculous times of night, the more so because he told me he didn't sleep. 'It's a waste of time, sleep. What do you achieve by sleeping? Nothing!' So he would read the papers. He would get a whole batch of papers and read them and construct his act for the next night. No contract was ever forthcoming, and it was quite the most bizarre incident, so I never got round to writing with Jackie Mason.

Jackie's career was nearly ruined because he incurred the wrath of Frank Sinatra. He told me he carried on working, but he wasn't getting the jobs he used to get and he wasn't earning the money he used to get, but still he carried on working. When Frank Sinatra married Mia Farrow, Jackie would be doing jokes like 'Imagine that, she's getting into bed with the brace on the teeth, he's taking off the wig and putting the teeth in the glass and getting up early in the morning to take her to school,' and Mr Sinatra was not amused by this. So Jackie told me how one night he'd been appearing in a club and he was staying in a motel close by and he said, 'Middle of the night I get up to take a leak, I go in the bathroom, boom, boom, shots,' and there were bullet holes in his pillow – somebody had shot through the window. This is vouched for. That night he went on at this club where he was appearing – this man knows no fear. He said to the audience, 'You hear about me today?' and then he told the story about going to the bathroom and everything and the bullets in the pillow, and he said, 'I go back in the room and the guy's running away, I've no idea who he was, all I could hear was him going "doobedoobedoo".'

Warm-ups were very good to me years ago. One year I earned more from warm-ups, which weren't that well paid, than I did from writing. Things were not too good at the time. I was briefly the warm-up man for Monty Python, as I've mentioned, but I did many other warm-ups, including a show with Harry H. Corbett, who'd risen to glory in *Steptoe and Son*, but was poached afterwards by London Weekend Television. Harry, who I knew, took me on one side and said, 'Barry, when you introduce me to the audience, before we start recording, please don't mention Steptoe.' 'Well,' I thought, 'this will be a bit of a challenge but, fair enough, I'll just mention his name, the audience know who he is.' I then did my introduction and said 'Harry H. Corbett', and over the speakers came the theme tune of *Steptoe*, and Harry's face fell.

In an episode of the series, which was called *Mr H* and was written by Galton and Simpson, no less, there appeared a performer called Eddie Gray. Now this is a name from the past, of a comedy juggler and eccentric comedian who worked with the Crazy Gang a lot, a notorious practical joker. I'm not a great fan of practical jokes if they're just cruel, but if they deflate somebody pompous, that's a different matter, then they can be vastly enjoyable. Eddie Gray, who I'd never met and was a bit in awe of, was playing a small part in this episode, and we were sitting having a cup of tea one day and there was a young, very intense actor sitting next to me, and Eddie Gray looked at me and there was almost a shadow of a wink and he said, 'Barry, have you heard anything about the dance?'

So I picked up on this and said, 'Not a word, Eddie, not a word.'

And he said, 'Well, it's a liberty, we haven't got a choreographer or anything. I'm not a dancer. Are you?' and I said, 'I certainly am not.' Then the young actor said, 'Sorry, sorry, what's this, what's this?' and Eddie said, 'Well, in the restaurant scene, we're all dancing. I mean there's been no preparation, nothing's been mentioned.' The actor said, 'I didn't know anything about this,' and Eddie said, 'None of us did. I think it's disgraceful!'

Later on I saw the actor accosting Chris Hodson, the director, who had been primed quietly by Eddie, and asking him, 'What's this about the dance?'

Chris said, 'I'm a bit busy at the moment. Later, later.' And this went on for, oh, a couple of hours. There was an element of cruelty in it, but Eddie Gray's practical jokes did at least show imagination. He was alleged to have invented the one where you stand talking into the mouth of a post or pillar box, as people go by, saying, 'Well, yes, I'll ring the fire brigade. How long have you been in there?' Then there's the one where you look up intently into the sky

186

and get other people to join you in gazing up, and when a crowd is gathered, all gazing upwards, you just walk away and leave them. He also gave a man in the street one end of a piece of string, telling him that he was a surveyor, and could he hold that for a moment, then went round the corner, handed the other end of the string to another man with the same story and then just left them. He probably wouldn't get to see the result, of course, but he was getting some strange satisfaction from imagining the situation that had occurred, even if he wasn't there to see it.

The warm-up lineage continues. Brian Conley, now a name in his own right, used to do the warm-ups for *The Kenny Everett Show* and subsequently appeared in a show called *Jolson*, based on the life of Al Jolson. One night, while they were doing the show, a couple were having it away, shall I say, in a box, almost in view of the audience, and Brian swears he caught sight of them as he was singing 'California Here I Come'.

When I was a stagehand at the Leeds Empire, I would always take a moment or two to try and talk to the artists, and I met idols of mine like Max Wall and comedians like Jimmy James, Terry-Thomas and goodness knows who else, as well as Chris Barber and his Band, who are still going strong, I'm happy to say. When skiffle erupted, Chris rather shrewdly created a skiffle group within the band, led by his guitarist/banjo player, Lonnie Donegan, and we all know what happened. Lonnie became an enormous star with 'Rock Island Line' and other records, and over the years he and I used to meet from time to time. Many years had gone by and I did a BBC programme called *I've Got a Secret*, the title of which is self-explanatory. People would come on, clues would be given and we on the panel had to guess what their secret was. So a man came on the programme one night and the clues involved very arch references to Barry Cryer's rubbish and so on, implying that's what I wrote or what I did. Anyway, we didn't get this man's secret, and he finally divulged that he was one of the dustmen in Hatch End, where I live. He said, 'I don't mind that you didn't recognise me – I'm the driver,' after which all the lads from the dust crew came on. Then a washboard was produced. I guess they'd been reading my CV, or else somebody had told them that many years before I used to play the washboard with the Leeds University Jazz Band. They produced thimbles, which you put on your fingers to play the washboard, and then Lonnie Donegan walked on and we all did 'My Old Man's a Dustman'. Cheers, Lonnie.

Back in the Seventies I worked on a show called *Who Do You Do?* consisting entirely of impressionists, look-alikes and sound-alikes. And one of the great characters was Joan Turner, the possessor of an amazing singing voice who could hit a high F or whatever and was often compared to a singer called Yma Sumac, whose real name was originally Amy Camus (but that's another story), who could also hit amazingly high notes. The last I heard of Joan was she was in the role of a bag lady in America. This was denied by her family, but we won't go down that road. One of the early emergents from that show (if there is such a word) was Freddie Starr, who became a star on a Royal Variety Performance. He was a brilliant man, who was doing impressions of Adam Faith and Billy Fury when they were already dated and also an impression of Adolf Hitler, who was fairly dated but, unfortunately, timeless.

Freddie was an amazing man. He was a rebel, a maverick, a loose cannon, a black sheep. My old friend Dick Vosburgh and I were editing the show on paper, and we used to bust our telephone bills by editing the show over the phone at night. We had thirteen shows per series, and Freddie, who was emerging as the absolute genius of the show, was very hard to spread around – his contribution was relatively thin but he was brilliant. So we sweated a lot on trying to get him into every show, but he never understood the logistics of this. Old professionals like Peter Goodwright and Janet Brown, brilliant impressionists, understood that they were regular members of the repertory company and that some nights they wouldn't have much to do but they'd be in the whole series. Freddie never understood this. One Friday night he only had three little bits to do, but he knew he was emerging as the star of the series, so that evening he sulked. There was one moment where he had to go on and do a very short joke in front of the audience, but instead of doing the joke he walked past the camera to the studio audience and faced them and said, 'I'm the fucking star of this show! You'd never know it tonight, would you?' The producer, John Scoffield, said to the floor manager, 'Get him in!' and Freddie was brought into the gallery to face the wrath of John Scoffield, who slammed him against the wall and said, 'Go home, little boy, and come back tomorrow and work!' When he came back, he was arrogant in his humility – it was quite alarming. He went from one person to another, including the whole camera crew and Dick Vosburgh, me and the other writers, shaking hands and saying, 'You're used to working with professionals – I'm a c***,' and Dick Vosburgh said, 'I'm frightened. I knew where I was with the old Freddie.'

I'm a devotee of public transport. I don't drive. I took lessons years ago and I had a very bad psychologist as an instructor because on the third lesson he took me on the Edgware Road and Kilburn High Road during the rush hour, and when the third bus loomed up I said, 'That's me out of here.' A very selfish decision. So I've never driven, therefore I'm a bit of a connoisseur of, not to say authority on, public transport. At my age I can remember going to school on a tram. I'm a big fan of trams – they're ecologically sound, environmentally utterly praiseworthy, no fumes, and they're not suddenly going to pull out. Years ago Yorkshire Television did a sort of rip-off of *Jim'll Fix It* for adults and did a ring-round asking if anybody had unfulfilled ambitions, and I don't know where it came from – the back of my brain, I suppose – but I said, 'I want to drive a tram.' They were quite intrigued and said they would fix it. So I thought it would be Blackpool or a museum or whatever, but no, they flew me to Amsterdam for a weekend and we were going to do the tram-driving on the Sunday. So I thought, 'What's happening on the Saturday?'

They asked me to do a little bit of filming on a bridge over one of the canals, and as I was talking on camera a man appeared from nowhere and said, 'Barry, come with me,' and whisked me away à la *This Is Your Life*. They took me to a place called Medemblik, where there were steam trains and fervent amateurs in greasy, oil-stained overalls. There was a university professor there with his face all black, and I drove a steam train from Medemblik to Hoorn, shovelling the coal in. I was in a state of ecstasy, it was unbelievable – all this and a tram as well. At one point I climbed along the side of the loco waving a flag as we approached a level crossing. That was great.

Next day was the day of the tram. Their modern trams are all computerised, and the driver's seat is akin to that of an airline pilot, surrounded by equipment, but mine wasn't one of those. They produced from their museum a tram which had run during the German occupation, with the brass handles and the 'ting ting' as you banged your foot on the floor, and I drove it one Sunday in Amsterdam. I nearly hit a white Porsche, but that's another story. I always say that my only unfulfilled ambition is to eat a prawn sandwich without the prawns falling out, but driving that tram was absolute nostalgia.

Talking of trams, said the butterfly brain, years ago there was a legendary comedian called Frank Randle, enormously popular in the north of England, the Doddy of his day. If he was going well he'd stay on till after midnight telling jokes. The relevance to trams is that he was a genuine eccentric, not to mention dangerously mad, and he once drove his car up the track straight at a tram shouting, 'Get out of the way.' Comedy was very regional in those days, before the onset of television, and comedians in the south could have a struggle up north and vice versa, and the great Randle came south to appear at the Finsbury Park Empire in London, and the audience did not take to him. They didn't understand him, they didn't like him and they began to stamp and even throw coins. Then the management inflicted on him the ultimate humiliation. They used to have (and still have in some theatres) a big fire curtain, known as 'the iron' in those days, and if an actor was really going beyond the pale or having a bad time they would humiliate him by dropping this curtain in front of him, thereby removing him from the sight of the audience, and this is what they did to Randle that night. But he ducked underneath, looked at the audience and shouted 'Bastards!'

Now there was a woman called Cissie Williams, known affectionately as The Godmother, who oversaw the Moss Empire's music halls. Frank Randle's conduct was reported to her by the manager at Finsbury Park, and Randle was summoned to her office to explain himself. Randle, a rather distinguished-looking man with a mane of silver hair, turned up, immaculate, in Cissie Williams' office and began to chat, and she said to him, 'You swore at the audience last night, Mr Randle, at Finsbury Park. We cannot countenance this.' 'No, no, my dear, never, never,' he replied. She braced herself and said the word that he'd shouted at the audience, to which Randle replied, 'My dear, have you the Italian?' and she said, 'What?' and he said, 'Have you the Italian? I was shouting at them, "Basta, basta – enough, enough."'

The great French singer Charles Aznavour was appearing in a show we were working on at Thames Television at Teddington, and we ate together in the restaurant at the studio. It turned out that Charles liked nothing better than a proper Sunday lunch of roast beef and gravy, with potatoes, Yorkshire pudding and all the trimmings. There was a waitress who couldn't take her eyes off him, and it transpired that she was going off duty and she was desperate to get his autograph. So she said to him, 'Mr Aznavour?'

'Yes, my dear,' he replied, and she very shyly and delightfully asked him for his autograph, and he said he would be delighted. He asked for her name and proceeded to autograph his Yorkshire pudding, digging the ballpoint pen in, and gave it to the waitress wrapped in a serviette, and I always imagine she kept it. Kept it until it became like concrete and finally crumbled away.

Postscript

Well, that's it – the end of a stream of unconsciousness. A daisy chain of irrelevance, a necklace of non sequitur. I can reveal that this book was written while exploring the new directory enquiries system and any accruing royalties can go towards my phone bill. I await further tirades from Oliver Roberts, who I heard recently was mistaken for Lord Lucan and now appears as a judge on *Fame Academy*. I should like to thank everyone who helped in the writing of this tome, especially Ainsley Harriott. Every time he came on television, I left the room and wrote another chapter. I am currently touring in an underwater version of *The Hunchback of Notre Dame* entitled *Ringing in the Seine*. I thank you for your patronage – I will be signing copies of this book at the Millennium Dome at midnight on April 1st. Unsigned copies will incur a 10% surcharge. I leave you now, as I'm taking my overdraft for a walk.

Yours obsequiously
B. Cryer (Mrs)

also available from
THE ORION PUBLISHING GROUP

All Orion/Phoenix titles are available at your local bookshop or from the following address:

Mail Order Department
Littlehampton Book Services
FREEPOST BR535
Worthing, West Sussex, BN13 3BR
telephone 01903 828503, *facsimile* 01903 828802
e-mail MailOrders@lbsltd.co.uk
(Please ensure that you include full postal address details)

Payment can be made either by credit/debit card (Visa, Mastercard, Access and Switch accepted) or by sending a £ Sterling cheque or postal order made payable to *Littlehampton Book Services*.
DO NOT SEND CASH OR CURRENCY.

Please add the following to cover postage and packing

UK and BFPO:
£1.50 for the first book, and 50p for each additional book to a maximum of £3.50

Overseas and Eire:
£2.50 for the first book plus £1.00 for the second book and 50p for each additional book ordered

---

BLOCK CAPITALS PLEASE

name of cardholder _____

delivery address
(if different from cardholder)

address of cardholder _____

_____

_____

postcode _____   *postcode* _____

☐ I enclose my remittance for £ _____

☐ please debit my Mastercard/Visa/Access/Switch (delete as appropriate)

card number ⬚⬚⬚⬚⬚⬚⬚⬚⬚⬚⬚⬚⬚⬚⬚⬚

expiry date ⬚⬚⬚⬚   Switch issue no. ⬚⬚

signature _____

prices and availability are subject to change without notice

WOMEN AND ECONOMICS